The
$25,000.00
Challenge

The $25,000.00 Challenge

World's
Toughest
Trivia Test

Ronald P. Smolin
&
Anthony T. Notaro

BainBridgeBooks
Philadelphia

Published October 1998
by
BainBridgeBooks
an imprint of
Trans-Atlantic Publications Inc.
Philadelphia PA

Website address: www.transatlanticpub.com

ISBN: 1-891696-03-3

Library of Congress # 98-93511

Cover and book design by
Graphic Decisions, Inc.

Send entries by
certified, return-receipt mail to:

TRIVIA CHALLENGE
BainBridgeBooks
311 Bainbridge Street
Philadelphia PA 19147-1543

Acknowledgements

The authors stand on the shoulders of all those past and present who have contributed to the wealth of ideas, projects, works of art, inventions, physical performances, and the entire range of activities that make civilization worthwhile.

We are indebted to many people who have contributed to this book, and we especially give thanks to:

Lawrence Cuthbert, Oliver from Germany, Chris from Saskatchewan, Louise Penman, Jerry from Kansas, Joseph Lukefajy from Texas, Christina E. Ziegler from Illinois, Michael D. Todd from South Carolina, Ashley Meredith from Kentucky, Corinne from Brisbane, Elvis from Maine, Charles McCown from Kentucky, Mike from San Francisco, Malc from Northern Ireland, Jake from "Out East," Jane the historian from Canada, Ryan Creagh from New Jersey, Dave Gallant from Prince Edward Island, Joyce Kain, Jeroen from the Netherlands, M. Cornelissen from the Netherlands, Rich Smart from Nevada, Susan Grace from England, Roze from Missouri, Jeremy Spencer from Tennessee, Grace Cameron from Nevada, Benjamin Maxfield from Massachusetts, Keith Blakey from England, Krissy Stone, Peter Glaze from Pennsylvania, Tanita Tikaram for her lyrics, John P. Hunt from ISI, to L. Chudd for signing Fats Domino, to Kismet for Fate's a Thing Without a Head, for Brahms in 1880, for the trombones in Beethoven's Fifth, W. Lane Startin from Warminster, to the Clockwork Orange Juice man, to Lovelock's Earth healing concept, to Bill McCollum and his concern about cyber predators, to Nicephore Soglo from the World Bank, Jeff and Bev Goldstein from Huntingdon Valley, Robert Simon of Philadelphia, to the abso-bloody-lutely difficult tmesis, to Jiffy & arachibutyrophobiacs, and to O.J. Simpson, who did make the covers of *Time*, *Newsweek*, and *Sports Illustrated*.

Contents

Quick Facts:

- There are no entry fees to play the Challenge
- Contest ends on September 12, 2000
- You may enter as a group or as an individual
- Enter in any or all categories
- A passing grade requires 60% or more correct answers and earns you a Trivia Challenge Certificate of Excellence
- If you get all the questions in all categories correct, you win $25,000.00 (or share it with anyone else getting all the questions correct)
- If no one answers all the questions correctly, six entrants qualify for a total of $15,000.00 in prize money if they can answer more than 60% of the questions in the entire Challenge.
- You have the option of donating all or a part of your winnings to your favorite charity
- Updates and hints will be posted on our website located at www.transatlanticpub.com

Introduction

We challenge you, whether as an individual or as a group, to engage in this difficult but potentially rewarding task of answering a wide range of trivia and general knowledge questions covering the vast panoply of human endeavor, from entertainment and the arts, to history, geography, sports, leisure, and science & technology.

In an era greatly influenced by physical fitness and the passivity of TV watching, we wanted to bring forth a challenge of Herculean proportion, where the mind finally gets a tough workout. Taking and passing this test will no doubt add years to your cognitive life and vitalize your intellectual aura!

Since the entry deadline is September 12, 2000, you will have considerable time to complete the Challenge, so do not let the number of questions intimidate you. Depending upon when you begin, all you need to answer is a few each day, combining research and your own ingenuity. To pass this test, you must answer at least 60% of the questions correctly; i.e., 940 or more correct of the 1,566 total.

In this Challenge, you have the option of donating all or a portion of your winnings to a charitable, educational, or other nonprofit organization.

There are eight categories of written questions and one category of Photo Challenge questions. You will also find some fill-in-the-blank questions as well as questions that ask you to provide the next line from a song. You can enter in any or all of the categories. Beat everyone else in any particular category and receive our Trivia Challenge Certificate of Excellence for that subject.

Throughout the book, you will find DID YOU KNOW? sections, which are not part of the contest, but which contain some interesting and often times humorous bits of information.

If you answer all the questions correctly in all categories, we will be pleased and astonished that someone or some group could accomplish this feat, and you will receive (or share if others tie you) the grand prize of $25,000.00.

Should no one answer all the questions correctly, then a new prize tier is available, including $10,000.00 for the most correct answers in all categories, when 60% or more are correct. There are also five $1,000.00 prizes for the runners-up.

We hope it's not only the money you're after but also the challenge and the reward from learning new information, honing your skills and applying your intelligence.

Hints to some answers are located in the book. The website will occasionally offer hints, so check the site at least once a month. (If you do not have access to the Internet, write the Publisher.) Please read the contest rules and official entry form carefully.

We wish you success in this most difficult challenge.

Ronald P. Smolin and Anthony T. Notaro
Philadelphia, August 1998

RULES OF THE TRIVIA CHALLENGE

(See complete list of rules on the Official Entry Form
found at the back of this book.)

THERE ARE NO FEES TO ENTER THIS CONTEST

1. This Challenge is open to anyone, in any country, other than owners or employees of BainBridgeBooks, Trans-Atlantic Publications, or
Coronet Books, subcontractors, and their family and friends.

2. The deadline for submitting your answers is September 12, 2000,
and thus all entries must be postmarked no later than that date.
Entries must be sent by registered, return receipt mail to ensure that
we receive your entry. You will be assigned a Challenge Number by
return mail.

3. All entries must contain the following:

a) The official entry form found in this book. (No photocopies are
allowed.)

b) A typed or computer-generated list of your answers, with the
letter & question number preceding your responses. Photo answers
must be preceded by "PC" and the number. You can enter any or all
of the categories. No handwritten entries are permitted. (Electronic
submission is not permitted as this medium is not completely safe.)

c) Your name, address and/or the organization you represent.
(This information will not be used for any purposes other than to contact you if you win any of the prizes. We will not divulge nor sell your
personal information to anyone, any group or any mail order firm.)

d) If you are submitting your responses on behalf of a group of
people who are participating in the Challenge with you, then each
member of the group must submit an official entry form, which
should then be collected and stapled or banded together. (This is
required to prevent any legal problems arising from allocating prize
money to your group.) The top entry form must have your name as

group leader. You have the option of providing us a unique name for your Challenge group.

e) If you wish to receive a list of all the answers, please enclose $2.00 to cover costs. This answer list will be mailed to you about 14 days after the entry deadline. The results of the contest will be posted on the website with a listing of all Entry numbers (and your optional Challenge name) and the number of correct responses. If you do not wish to have your actual name posted, we will list only your Challenge number and/or fictitious name.

4. Any one person or group getting all questions correct will receive the grand prize of $25,000.00 paid over a five year period, that is, $5,000.00 per year beginning January 2001.

5. If there are ties for getting all the questions correct, the prize money of $25,000.00 will be shared equally by the winners, and paid over a five year period.

6. If no one answers all questions correctly, the entry with the most correct responses (with at least 60% of all questions answered correctly) will receive a $10,000.00 prize, paid over a two year period, that is, $5,000.00 per year beginning January 2001.

7. If there are ties for getting the greatest number correct, the prize money of $10,000.00 will be divided equally and paid over a two-year period.

8. In addition to the $10,000.00 prize, the Publisher will award cash prizes of $1,000.00 to the five runners-up, i.e., to those coming in 2nd, 3rd, 4th, 5th, and 6th places. (Remember, to qualify for any cash prize, you must answer at least 60% of all the questions correctly.)

9. Anyone or any group getting 60% or more correct answers receives a Trivia Challenge Certificate of Excellence. A Certificate is also awarded to those scoring the most points in any particular category.

10. The results of the Challenge will be posted on our website approximately one month after the contest ends. The correct answers will be posted on or about December 1, 2000. The website address is www.transatlanticpub.com. If you do not have access to the Internet, write the Publisher.

11. Questions were developed during 1998. Because the Challenge runs for about two years, certain answers may be affected during this time period. After receiving the answers to the Challenge, if you believe you have a more up-to-date response to the question or a challenge to our answer and have documentation to that effect, you may issue a claim by sending a registered letter to the Publisher at:

Trivia Challenge, BainBridgeBooks
311 Bainbridge Street,
Philadelphia PA 19147-1543

Include the question number, your response, and your documentation supporting your claim. All claims must reach the Publisher no later than December 31, 2000.

12. Should no disputes affect the outcome of the Challenge, the first payment to the winners will be made in January 2001. If disputes do occur, payment will be made upon settlement of any and all disputes.

13. If your answer to a question is partially correct, the Publisher may award you partial credit. Full names are required in the answer if the last name is not unique. All answers should be spelled correctly. We will not penalize for an obvious typographical error in your answer to a question.

14. You may also enter the Challenge on behalf of a charitable or non-profit organization, allocating all or a portion of your winnings to such entities. If so, please mark the official entry form in this book, indicating what organization you are playing for and what percentage of the winnings you wish to allocate.

15. Please be aware that the material in this book is under copyright protection. Copying parts of this book is illegal and will result in disqualification from the contest.

Begin The Challenge . . .

A: POPULAR ENTERTAINMENT

Film
TV
Music
Theater

Did You Know?

- The word "trivia" comes from the Latin "trivium," which was the place where three roads met at a public square. People would gather and talk about all sorts of matters, most of which were trivial.

- According to the World Health Organization, there are approximately 100 million acts of sexual intercourse each day.

- More money is printed daily for the game of Monopoly than money printed by the US Treasury Department.

- The use of a period after Mr, Mrs, Jr and Dr is not correct. To shorten a word, a period is used only to indicate that the next letters in the words are truncated. Street takes a period, St., because the 'reet' have been dropped; but Saint should be St—without a period—since the first and last letters have been combined. Thus doctor and mister should be Dr or Mr—and so on.

A1. Who was the only cast member of *M*A*S*H* to have actually served in the Korean War?

A2. What pop group starts a song by singing the word "Go" at least seventy-two times in a row?

A3. Viagra would have helped what character in *sex, lies & videotape*?

A4. How tall was the model ape in the 1933 movie *King Kong*?

A5. What sitcom character wore a Band-aid in every episode?

A6. What radio and then TV program started off with, "Ladies and gentlemen, the story you are about to hear is true. Only the names have been changed to protect the innocent?"

A7. Fill in the blanks to find out what movie character says: "I don't like violence, Tom. I'm a businessman. Blood is a big expense."

$$\_ \_ L L \_ \_ \_$$

A8. What is the origin of the good-luck phrase of actors, "break a leg?"

A9. The *Perry Mason* TV series was based upon the novels of what writer?

A10. Which group sang these lyrics:
"A boy tries hard to be a man,
His mother takes him by the hand,
If he stops to think he starts to cry.
Oh why?"

A11. What film's opening scenes show a man collapsing while watering his lawn and a billboard stating "Welcome to Lumberton?"

A12. Mike is a narcoleptic street hustler in what film?

A13. Fill in the blanks to discover who did not win an Oscar for his brilliant performance playing Mozart.

$$\_ \_ M \qquad \_ \_ L \_ E$$

A14. What long running private eye TV show starred Efrem Zimbalist, Jr and Roger Smith?

A15. What TV show had the personal endorsement of J. Edgar Hoover?

A16. At what age did Ray Charles lose his sight?

A17. Which two members of Crosby, Stills, Nash & Young were not born in the USA?

A18. What does M.G. stand for in the name Booker T. & the M.G.s?

A19. What film, running 2:05, starts with a man brandishing a flame-thrower on an L.A. street?

A20. What kind of cigarettes does James Bond smoke?

A21. Whose badge number is 2211?

A22. What film, based upon actual events, begins in the Comoros Islands, East Africa, in July 1983?

A23. Raymond Burr played an ex-San Francisco chief of detectives in what TV show?

A24. Who played the TV actor known for his expression, "Who loves ya, baby?"

A25. "Hartley's homilies" were part of which TV show?

A26. Fill in the blanks to find the name of a rotund comic Tony winner:
_ E _ _   _ _ S T _ _

A27. What Broadway musical is based upon the music of Alexander Borodin?

A28. Who is Issur Danielovitch Demsky?

A29. In what cartoon did Daffy Duck make his 1937 debut?

A30. What were the first movie and sequel to be released in the same year?

A31. In what film does a satellite fall to earth in a remote New Mexico village, killing everyone except an infant and an old derelict?

A32. What is the full name of the Skipper on *Gilligan's Island*?

A33. Who has the only speaking role in *Silent Movie*?

A34. What backup singer on Guns n' Roses' *Use Your Illusion* died after releasing an album with his own band?

A35. What are the names of the two New Jersey-born comedians whose first Broadway show was *The Streets of Paris*?

A36. What was the first cartoon character to have ever been made into a balloon for a parade?

A37. On what album cover can one find the license plate 281F?

A38. Who appeared in a Disney film and on the 1875 $20 bill?

A39. Fill in the blanks to find out what the last shot of the day is called in film production.

   _ H _   _ A _ T _ N _   _ H _ _

A40. What was the title of the first episode of *The Munsters*?

A41. What TV character said, "You see that guy over there? Now, he's an actor. The guy on the phone? He's a prizefighter. This lady over here? She's a beautician. The man behind her? He's a writer. Me? I'm a cab driver?"

A42. What was the title of the first *Welcome Back, Kotter* episode?

Did You Know?

- More than 1,000 floppy disks can be stored on one CD-ROM.

- More than 37,000 black soldiers lost their lives during the Civil War.

- The average hospital launders about 52,000 pounds of linen each week.

- Some 1500 slaughterhouses in the USA produce 39 billion pounds of meat each year.

- Most petroleum is located in about 700 sedimentary rock basins throughout the world, and about half of these have been at least partially explored and drilled.

- Every 1.5 seconds someone catches a sexually transmitted disease.

A43. On what TV show will you find the Narn Regime and the Vorlon Empire?

A44. How many ships were there in the caravan that tagged along *Battlestar Galactica*?

A45. In what film, based upon a Broadway play, do we hear this monologue:

> "I think my biggest problem is being young and beautiful. It's my biggest problem because I've never been young and beautiful. Oh, I've been beautiful. God knows I've been young. But never the twain have met."

A46. What's the population of the fictional Garrison, New Jersey?

A47. How long is the song, "Add it Up," by a Milwaukee-based group?

A48. Which group sang these lyrics:

"I booked myself in at the Y...WCA,
I said: "I like it here—can I stay?...
And, do you have a vacancy
For a Back-Scrubber?"

A49. What was the first word spoken by an ape in *Planet of the Apes*?

A50. How much did Ralph Cramden earn per week?

A51. Fill in the blanks to the four-word song title and tell us who sang it:

$$D \_\_\ ' \_$$
$$\_ O\ R \_\_ ,$$
$$\_ E \quad \_ A \_\_ Y$$

A52. What four Broadway musicals were the only ones to tie for a Tony Award?

A53. From what Italian surrealistic and "spiritual" film will you find this dialogue:

"The master himself will tell you."

"It's an apple ... it's only an apple ... a humble little apple ... small and red ... and bruised on one side. But at the same time it's the Buddha and the single spirit. Things return to being things but the Illuminated sees at the same time Oneness and Manyness ... sees appearance as well as substance."

A54. NEXT LYRIC LINE PLEASE:

You wake up in the middle of the night,
Your sheets are wet and your face is white,
You tried to make a good thing last,
How could something so good, go bad, so fast?

A55. What is the name of the song whose sub-title is: "Or How I Was Robert McNamara'd into Submission?"

A56. What Chicago Academy of Fine Arts' cartoonist taught Walt Disney?

A57. What is the first crime mentioned in the first episode of *Hill Street Blues*?

A58. What is Donald Duck's address?

A59. How many minutes of new footage were in the new release of *Star Wars*?

A60. Respectively, what are the real first names of Chico, Harpo, Groucho, and Zeppo Marx?

A61. Why is R2-D2 so named?

A62. Fill in the blanks to find out who created the comic strip *Popeye* in 1919?

     _ L _ I _   _ R I _ _ E R   _ E _ _ R

A63. Who does the voices for Miss Piggy, Fozzie Bear and Yoda?

A64. In the *Lone Ranger*, what was the name of Tonto's horse?

A65. What member of the Beatles was born during a WWII air raid?

A66. What was the first song played on Armed Forces Radio during "Desert Storm?"

A67. From what film will you find this monologue:

"No man alive can resist that and that's why I got in the jail to begin with and they're telling me I'm crazy over here ´cause I don't sit like a goddamn vegetable. Don't make a bit of sense to me. If that's what being crazy is then I'm senseless, out of it, gone down the road whacko. But no more no less."

A68. What was Elvis Presley's twin brother's name?

A69. Fill in the blanks to find out which muscleman received 2000 fan letters a week for his portrayal of a TV hulk:

_ O _   F _ _ R _ G _ _

A70. In a TV sci-fi series, what was KITT and what do the letters stand for?

A71. In *Lost in Space*, the TV series, who played the Robot and who provided the Robot's voice?

A72. In what TV series did fictional characters Tony Newman and Doug Phillips work miles under the surface of the Arizona desert?

A73. What was the first comic book published for newsstand sales in 1934?

A74. Fill in the blanks to discover the name of the spaceship on TV's *Lost in Space*:

_ _ P _ T _ _   _

A75. Who is Annie Mae Bullock?

A76. Who provided the voice of the narrator in *The Texas Chainsaw Massacre*?

Did You Know?

- Tom Cruise's real name is Tom Mapother. Vanilla Ice is Robert Van Winkle. Burning Spear is Winston Rodney. Rita Hayworth is Margarita Casino. Captain Beefheart is Don Van Vliet. WANG CHUNG are Jack Hues and Nick Feldman. Pat Benetar is Patricia Andrzejewski. Elton John is Reginald Dwight. Elvis Costello is Declan McManus. David Bowie is David Jones.

- The longest chapter in the Bible is Psalm 19.

- About 2-4% of the Internet contains sex sites, yet they account for up to 20% of the search requests!

A77. What was Spock's blood type on *Star Trek*?

A78. Who plays piano on the theme song for the show *Mad About You*?

A79. What band was originally called the Warlocks?

A80. In what film that takes place in the 1930s do we find a butler unable to express his feelings towards the estate's housekeeper, while standing by his master who is duped by the Nazis?

A81. What do the following people have in common: John Benjamin Hickey, Denis O'Hare, and Sam Mendes?

A82. Name the film produced by Scott Rudin, directed by Peter Weir, and edited by William Anderson.

A83. Kurt Russell and Ernest Borgnine teamed up in what 1981 film?

A84. NEXT LYRIC LINE PLEASE:
> The preacher talked with me and he smiled; said:
> "Come and walk with me, come on walk one more mile;
> now for once in your life you're alone
> But you ain't got a dime
> there's no time for the phone."

A85. Who created the comic strip *Andy Capp*?

A86. Fill in the blanks to find out who starred in the film *Sherlock Jr*?
    _ _ S T _ _   _ _ A T _ _

A87. What is vocal sampling?

A88. In what film does a starving female singer in Depression-era Paris pass herself off as a man?

A89. What is the name of the concerts organized by Adam Yauch of the Beastie Boys to raise public concern about the Dalai Lama & the people of Tibet?

A90. What are the two melody types in Hindu music?

A91. In what film will you find the following dialogue:
> "Ronnie, maybe a little trip is all you need. The place down in Mexico you were talking about."
>
> "I want to go no place."
>
> "Ronnie, I think you should go. What can I do, Ronnie? What do you want?"
>
> "I want to be a man again. Who's gonna love me, dad? Who's ever gonna love me?"

A92. Will Sergeant played lead guitar in what group in 1981?

A93. What's the full street address of *The Brady Bunch?*

A94. TV Detective Tony Baretta lived in what hotel?

A95. What car did Lt Columbo drive?

A96. *The Fugitive* was inspired by which real life case?

A97. What is the longest running crime series in the history of American TV?

A98. What are the two dinosaur-type vehicles that the Mighty Morphin Power Rangers used?

A99. Who wrote and sang the following lyrics:
> "I was a free man in Paris
> I felt unfettered and alive
> There was nobody calling me up for favors
> And no one's future to decide"

A100. In what group will you find Geddy Lee, Alex Lifeson and Neil Peart?

A101. Who wrote "It's Still Rock & Roll to Me" and "Sleeping with the Television On?"

A102. Opening at the Broadway Theater in New York on May 21, 1959, which Merrick-Hayward-Laurents-Styne-Sondheim musical ran for 702 performances?

A103. In what film will you hear these opening lines:
> "Norman, come here, come here ... The loons,
> the loons—they're welcoming us back."

A104. NEXT LYRIC LINE PLEASE:
> What about the boy?
> What about the boy?
> What about the boy?

A105. What jazz trumpeter won a Grammy Award for his work on the *First Light* album?

A106. How long does *Peaceful, Easy Feeling* last in its original recording?

A107. In the film, *Men in Black*, what was "J's" full name before all his records were deleted?

A108. In what film will you find the character President Skroob?

A109. In the USA, the film *Superman* runs for 143 minutes. How long does it run in Sweden?

A110. Mashed potatoes play an important part in what sci-fi film?

A111. What satiric TV series featured the Tate and Campbell sisters?

A112. What artist created *The Simpsons*?

A113. In what film will you hear the following dialogue:
> "Do you have such a thing as a reliable atlas?"
>
> "I believe so."
>
> "Excellent. I wish to check the position of the Nile. My sister tells me it's in South America."
>
> "Oh, no, no. She's quite wrong, for I believe it's in Belgium."

Did You Know?

Men think that women are just like computers because:

- No one but the Creator understands their internal logic.
- The language they use to communicate with other computers is incomprehensible to everyone else.
- The message "Bad Command" is about as informative as "If you don't know why I'm mad at you, I'm certainly not going to tell you."
- Your smallest mistakes are stored in long-term memory for later retrieval.
- As soon as you buy a computer you spend half your paycheck on accessories for it.

Women think that men are just like computers because:

- They have a ton of data but are still clueless.
- They are supposed to help you solve problems, but half the time they are the problem.
- As soon as you commit to one, you realize if you had waited a little longer, you could have obtained a better model.
- In order to get their attention, you have to turn them on.
- A big power surge will knock them out for the rest of the night!

A114. Fill in the blanks to discover which TV series was set at 165 Eaton Place, London.

_ _ S _ A _ _ _   _ _ _ N S _ _ I _ S

A115. Dr Joel Fleischmann worked in the town of Cicely, which had a population of how many people?

A116. What group contained the following people: Bjorn Ulvaeus, Agnetha Faltskog, Anni-Frid Lyngstad, and Benny Andersson?

A117. What famous British actor changed his name to honor his schoolmaster who helped him obtain a scholarship to Oxford University?

A118. What singer made it big in 1956 with "Please, Please, Please?"

A119. In 1998, what publicly traded company purchased more than 50% of the USA national concert promotion market, including concerts by the Eagles and Spice Girls?

A120. Whose 1966 Liverpool concert broke an attendance record previously set by the Beatles?

A121. Fill in the blanks to discover the name of this singer, guitarist, actor and band leader born in Liverpool in 1947:

_ E _ _ R   _ _ O N _

A122. What opened in Niblo's Gardens in New York City in 1866?

A123. Which handicapped musical child prodigy released his first record at the age of 13?

A124. In what year did the following soundtracks win Gold-record awards: *My Fair Lady*, *Carousel*, *King & I*, and *Mary Poppins*?

A125. What famous actor began working for the Karno vaudeville company when he was 17 years old?

A126. Which two people played "Dueling Banjos?"

A127. Which Hollywood producer owned the largest chain of motion-picture theaters in New England in 1918?

A128. What Texas-born singer, writer and actor won a Rhodes Scholarship to Oxford University and also wrote songs for Janis Joplin, Frank Sinatra, and Johnny Cash, among others?

A129. Who performed the song, "Parents Just Don't Understand?"

A130. The song, "Eye of the Tiger," appears in what film?

A131. Fill in the blanks to find this Oscar-winning song from the 1960s:

_ H _ M   C _ _ _   _ H E _ - _ _

A132. NEXT LYRIC LINE PLEASE:
"Every time I think I'm the only one who's lonely
Someone calls on me
And every now and then I spend my time at rhyme and verse
And curse those faults in me..."

A133. Who holds the 1969 copyright to *Tommy* (The Rock Opera)?

A134. What great jazz superstar got his first professional job with Eddie Randall's Blue Devils?

A135. Who wrote the song, "Oye Como Va?"

A136. In November 1925, what radio program eventually led to the creation of the Grand Ole Opry?

A137. On what album will you find a song about Binky the Doormat?

A138. How long is "Love is a Battlefield" in its original recording?

A139. NEXT LYRIC LINE PLEASE:

"Mamma!
Rockin' on the roulette wheel!
Mamma grabbed my hand
She was about to die
And she said ..."

A140. What Woody Allen film uses the music of Mendelssohn?

A141. Fill in the blanks to find the composer whose themes were used for *Flash Gordon* serials:

_ _ A N _   _ I _ _ T

A142. In what film will you hear the following monologue:

"I create nothing. I own. We make the rules, pal.
The news, war, peace, famine, upheaval, the price of
paper clip. We pick that rabbit out of the hat while
everybody sits out there wondering how the hell
we did it. Now you're not naïve enough to think
we're living in a democracy, are you, Buddy?"

A143. What song has the subtitle: "Take a Look at Me Now?"

A144. Who is the comic that produced an award winning album which satirized the JFK family?

A145. What group won the first MTV Best Video award?

A146. What pop group's song begins with these lyrics: "Day after day, I will work and I will play?"

A147. What was the name of the original pilot for TV's *Star Trek*?

A148. The original *USS Enterprise* had how many officers and crew?

Did You Know?

- TYPEWRITER is the longest English word that can be made using the letters on only one row of the keyboard.
- The "#" is called an octothorpe.
- In 1980, the yellow pages accidentally listed a Texas funeral home under Frozen Foods.
- Moses Maimonides, 10th century physician to the Egyptian Caliph, prescribed snow as a cure for the hot Cairo summers.
- In Ecuador there is a statue honoring poet José Olmedo. Unfortunately for the poet, the government could not afford to commission a sculptor, so instead bought a second-hand statue … of English poet Lord Byron!
- The word samba literally means to rub navels together.

A149. Who played "The Observer" Al Calavicci?

A150. What magical substance on Wonder Woman's bracelets gave her superhuman strength and deflected bullets?

A151. Who created *The X Files*?

A152. What's the name of the actual police precinct that provided the police station exterior shots in *Hill Street Blues*?

A153. What's the name of the NBC series that was the first major series to star a black actor on equal footing with a white one?

A154. Telly Savalas shaved his head for the first time for what Hollywood film?

A155. Who was the first person to win two consecutive Grammy awards for best album of the year?

A156. What group sang "Every Dog Has His Day?"

A157. What was the first Beatles song to win a Grammy?

A158. For what musical did Leonard Bernstein receive a Tony Award?

A159. The Tony awards are named for what person?

A160. Fill in the blanks to find what Thomas Heggen and Joshua Logan wrote:

_ I _ T _ _   _ _ _ E _ T S

A161. In the 1980s, what TV program won three Emmy Awards for best drama?

A162. In the 1970s, what TV program won three Emmy Awards for best drama?

A163. The National Academy of Television Arts & Sciences Awards first formed in what year?

A164. What was the first film to win an Oscar for best film in the foreign language category?

A165. Marvin Hamlisch wrote the score of what film produced by ITC Entertainment Presentation and Pakula-Barish Production?

A166. What famous actor was part of the acrobatic team of Lang & Cravat?

A167. Which well known singer, guitarist and songwriter formed his first group in St Louis with pianist Johnny Johnson and drummer Ebby Harding?

A168. Who wrote the song, "The Man Who Shot Liberty Valance?"

A169. "It's Uptown," released in 1965, featured the work of what Pittsburgh-born jazz guitarist?

A170. In 1957, Perry Mason relied on what private investigator to gather evidence and witnesses?

A171. Who won an Oscar for acting in *The Diary of Anne Frank*?

A172. Who wrote the first episode of *Bewitched*?

A173. The producers of the film *Star Wars* issued writs against which TV show, claiming plagiarism?

A174. On television, fictional Dr David Banner was injected with an overdose of what to become a green-skinned, man-beast of superhuman strength.

A175. Who is the 720-year old with two hearts from the planet Gallifrey?

A176. Fictional character Steve Austin was refurbished at a cost of $6 million by what doctor?

A177. What TV fictional character was originally to be called Captain April?

A178. In what movie is the following line, "Pardon me while I whip this out?"

A179. What Hawthorne, California, pop group's first smash hit was recorded on the Candix label?

A180. NEXT LYRIC LINE PLEASE:

"When you're weary, feeling small
When tears are in your eyes, I will dry them all;
I'm on your side. When times get rough
And friends just can't be found..."

A181. What was the first video ever aired on MTV Europe?

A182. The song, "Mean Green Mother from Outer Space," appears in what film?

A183. NEXT LYRIC LINE PLEASE:

"Like a perfume woman the wind blows in the bunk house.
Like a perfume woman smelling of where she's been,
smelling of Oregon cherries
or maybe Texas avocado
or maybe Arizona sugar,
the wind blows in and she sings to me
'cause I'm one of her kin. She sings:"

A184. What was the first PBS program to win an Emmy Award?

A185. Who was the first to win three consecutive Emmy Awards for best actor in a drama?

A186. Who received a best actor Emmy for *The Untouchables*?

A187. What special award did Gene Kelly receive in 1985?

A188. Louis Gossett Jr won an Oscar for what film?

A189. Timothy Hutton and Robert Redford won Oscars for what film?

Did You Know?

• On the TV series, Lassie played the part of a caring female dog and yet only male dogs were used in the role.

• Sir Arthur Conan Doyle's character Sherlock Holmes oddly resembles a detective character from an earlier work by Edgar Allen Poe. The character not only used deductive reasoning, was impossibly brilliant, and smoked a pipe, but his name was Sherlaw Kolms.
(Believe it or not — NOT!!)

• The US Declaration of Independence was printed on hemp paper.

• Only 9% of people 55 years of age and over use the Internet.

A190. Fill in the blanks to find the recipient of a Grammy for Best New Artist of the Year in 1982:

_ _ N   _ _   _ O _ _

A191. What song received the first Grammy for Best Country & Western Performance?

A192. Who are the two singers of the song, "Lover Please?"

A193. On what national television show did the first toilet bowl appear?

A194. Who was called the "statue of libido?"

A195. Who were Bert and Ernie named after on Sesame Street?

A196. Who were the only two classic Warner Brothers cartoon characters that Mel Blanc did not do the voices for?

A197. NEXT LYRIC LINE PLEASE:

"But that picture frame is the saddest thing you'll see;
well, it bought time and a place that love could be;
and since I'm going now please rearrange
'cause I'd like to think things have changed ..."

A198. What song are these lyrics from?

"... such a cold finger beckons you
to enter his web of sin—but don't go in!"

A199. What pop group sings about a "big old sweater," a "magic carpet high above the earth," and "Capricorn rising?"

A200. In what film's opening scenes do we see an accountant working in a funeral home and a florist shop and a woman in a restaurant throwing water onto the lap of her date and saying, "Kiss my aspirations!"

A201. The voices of some original members of the *Dirty Dozen* cast are used in what 1990s film?

A202. Three garrulous musicians met at the Rhode Island School of Design in the early 1970s to go on and form what quirky pop group?

A203. Who plays Lister on the TV series *Red Dwarf?*

A204. What pop group sings about cruising through the ionosphere and seeing alien beings everywhere shaking their honeybuns?

A205. In what musical will you find Officer Krupke?

A206. In what film will you hear this dialogue:

Ben: "There's a shooting star!"

Toomer: "There's no star, boy. That's the tear of infant Jesus falling on account of such a sinful and hateful world."

A207. In what film will you find the Rock Ridge Town Council?

A208. *Apocalypse Now* is partially based upon what novel?

A209. In the film *Copland*, what's the name of the bar in Garrison, New Jersey, where police officers meet?

A210. In what film will you hear the song, "Springtime for Hitler?"

A211. Chubby Checker is usually given credit for his hit, "The Twist," but who actually created this song?

A212. Which pop group was born in England in the 1940s and emigrated to Australia in 1958?

A213. Who brought the first circus to America?

A214. What were the names of the three Paul Butterfield series of bands?

A215. What famous singer was discovered by Harry James at the Rustic Cabin in New Jersey in 1939?

A216. What two actresses played Phyllis Lindstrom and Bess Lindstrom in one of TV's most popular comedy series?

A217. What is the longest-running science fiction series in TV history?

A218. The Stevie Wonder song, "I Just Called to Say I Love You," appeared in what film?

A219. *X-Files'* star David Duchovny played a transvestite FBI agent in what TV series?

A220. Who worked for the Syracuse University radio station and then got a job as a summer replacement at WFIL in Philadelphia in 1952?

A221. Called by Rolling Stone in 1970 "the finest, most precise bottleneck guitar player alive today," who is this person who first started playing at the Ash Grove?

A222. Lew Chudd, head of Imperial Records, signed which famous singer to a record contract while he was making $3 a week playing the piano at the Hideaway Bar in New Orleans in 1949?

A223. After being recorded on Columbia and Asylum record companies, who started his own firm called Ashes & Sand?

A224. Fill in the blanks to this five-word song from a British group which sold more than four million copies of it worldwide in 1967:

_   _ H I _ E R   _ H _ _ E
        O _   _ A L _

A225. Who sang these lyrics:
"Nightmares dreamed by bleeding men,
lookouts tremble on the shore
no man can find the war."

A226. What's the title of the song in which these lyrics are sung:
"Well we dance all night, play all day
Don't let nothin' get in the way;
We dance all night and keep the beat;
Don't you worry about two left feet."

Did You Know?

• The longest non-medical word in the English language is not antidisestablishmentarianism. Rather it is a word meaning the act or habit of estimating as worthless, and it is:

  Floccinaucinihilipilification

• The longest medical word in the English language is a lung disease. It is:

  Pneumonoultramicroscopicsilicovolcanoconiosis

  (We believe there are three people now alive who can pronounce it.)

A227. In what film does the hero move back and forth in time, sometimes on a distant planet, sometimes in WW II, and sometimes as an optometrist, living with his family?

A228. What TV crime and mystery series was known as *Chapeau Melon et Bottes de Cuir* in France and *Mit Schirm, Charm und Melone* in Germany?

A229. What fictional character drives a Lotus 7, registration number KAR 120C?

A230. How much did TV's Jim Rockford charge his clients?

A231. What fictional character has a calling card that depicts a stick figure with a halo?

A232. "Who killed Laura Palmer" was a central question in what TV series?

A233. Who lived 250 miles below sea level in Cobblestone Country?

A234. The A -Team was imprisoned for robbing which bank?

A235. Which musician started with the Pilgrim Travellers in the 1950s and issued his first LP in 1962 called *Stormy Monday*?

A236. Which Irish group produced the LP called *Shades of a Blue Orphanage*?

A237. What pop song was conceived during a breakfast of chicken and eggs?

A238. Who is the Buffalo-born musician who played the national anthem for the Philadelphia 76ers and Philadelphia Eagles and was a founding member of the Four Clefs?

A239. Ronnie Milsap and Kenny Rogers received a Grammy for Best Country Performance Duet for what song?

A240. Doc and Merle Watson received a Grammy for what song in 1979?

A241. In the 1980s, which female received two consecutive Grammy awards for Best Country Vocal Performance?

A242. Fill in the blanks of this four-word country music group and discover how you should never be found:

_ S _ _ _ P   _ _   _ _ E   _ _ E _ L

A243. Who wrote the song, "The Gambler?"

A244. Who performed "Just a Little Talk with Jesus?"

A245. Who composed the music for *The Godfather*?

 ENTRY DEADLINE: September 12, 2000

A246. Who wrote the lyrics to the song, "Raindrops Keep Fallin' on My Head?"

A247. What TV show has a 1,000-member crew aboard the *Enterprise*?

A248. What was the slogan of the Rock Head & Quarry Cave Construction Company?

A249. Michael Garrison created what TV series that included an inventor and master of disguise named Artemus Gordon?

A250. *The Lone Ranger* began life on what radio station and in what city?

A251. *Little House on the Prairie* was based upon whose books about life in the Old West?

A252. Fill in the blanks to find this character's name on a police TV comedy series:

_ H I _   _ I S _

A253. What is the name of a former TV producer and California state lottery winner who led a campaign to ban *Beavis & Butt-Head*?

A254. What is the name of the baby on the cover of Nirvana's *Nevermind*?

A255. What band got its name from a sexual device mentioned in a William S. Burroughs novel?

A256. What do *The Simpsons'* Sideshow Bob and *Les Miserables'* Jean Valjean have in common?

A257. What was the name of the musical group that game show host Chuck Woolery was part of and what was their top 40 hit?

A258. What pop star grew up on Simcoe Street in downtown Kingston?

A259. What is the only Pink Floyd song not sung by a member of the band and who sang it?

A260. What band got its name from the 1968 movie *Barbarella*?

A261. What popular song was written about Mia Farrow's sister?

A262. Who is the one and only person to have won an Oscar, a Tony, a Grammy, and an Emmy?

A263. NEXT LYRIC LINE PLEASE:

"I sat down feeling desolated,
bowed my head and crossed my knees;
is fortune predicated upon such tiny turns as these?
Then fate's a thing without a head—a puzzle never understood,
and man proceeds where he is led:"

A264. NEXT LYRIC LINE PLEASE:
"And the jailor man
and the sailor man
were searching everyone for:"

A265. In which TV show was Arnold's Drive-in?

A266. Which fictional family lived at 328 Chauncey Street, Brooklyn?

A267. What 1950s TV series was based at fictionalized Fort Baxter, Kansas?

Did You Know?

- In 1964, William F. Buckley Jr was asked what he thought of the Beatles. He said, "The Beatles are not merely awful, I would consider it sacrilegious to say anything less than they are godawful. They are so unbelievably horrible, so appallingly unmusical, so dogmatically insensitive to the magic of art, that they qualify as crowned heads of anti-music ..." (Source: *Cassell Dictionary of Insulting Quotations.*)

- The buttons on men's suits originated in Napoleon's army because the enlisted men regularly wiped their noses on their shirtsleeves.

- The yellow pus from infections is a collection of dead bacteria, dead white blood cells, and liquefied tissues.

- Those born with the rare disease called progeria appear normal at first, but within a few years age rapidly, developing a large head and a beaked nose. They lose their hair, usually have heart attacks by the age of 10, and die by the age of 15.

- The dimensions of the Compact Disc were determined in the following manner: Philips (the inventor) chose the diameter of a Dutch ten cent coin for the size of the hole in the CD; whereas Sony determined the outer diameter of the CD by the length of time for Beethoven's 9th Symphony (72 minutes long).

A268. What current movie star and current political figure were roommates at Harvard?

A269. Who was "Martha My Dear" written for?

A270. The song, "Moon River," appears in what film?

A271. Respectively, what are Jerry Seinfeld's and Kramer's apartment numbers?

A272. Who is O'Shea Jackson better known as?

A273. What Teenage Mutant Ninja Turtle is named after an artist from a different time period than the other three?

A274. What program did UPN inaugurate on January 16, 1995, with the episode called *Caretaker*?

A275. With an all-male crew, which fictional vessel did scientific research for the Nelson Institute of Marine Research?

A276. What was the name of the law firm on the TV series *LA Law*?

A277. In *The Man from UNCLE*, what did UNCLE stand for?

A278. Which two TV fictional characters worked for the Blue Moon Detective Agency?

A279. Which TV detective's offices were located at 351 Ellis Park Road in Los Angeles?

A280. NEXT LYRIC LINE PLEASE:
> "Lost feelings return
> So now maybe I can learn.
> Stop the world—I'm alive,
> This time around:"

A281. Which famous singer, guitarist and songwriter did his first public singing on radio station KLCN in Blytheville, Arkansas, when he was in high school?

A282. What well known singer and songwriter performed on the streets of Brooklyn in 1951 at the age of 10 with a group called the Memphis Backstreet Boys?

A283. In 1957, before the opening of one of the most successful Broadway musicals ever, who said, "I don't know how many people begged me not to waste my time on something that could not possibly succeed ... a show full of hatefulness and ugliness?"

A284. Who is the pop musician whom Elvis Presley called "the greatest singer in the world" and who toured with the Beatles in 1963?

A285. NEXT LYRIC LINE PLEASE:
"I met a strange lady,
she made me nervous.
She took me in and gave me breakfast.
She said:"

A286. In what film will you hear this monologue:
"Now let us dispel some rumors so they just don't fester into fact. Yes, I too attended Helton and survived. And no, at that time I was not the mental giant you see before you. I was the intellectual equivalent of a 98-pound weakling."

A287. Who wrote the song, "9-5?"

A288. "Babylon the Bandit" was performed by what group?

A289. Who was first offered the TV role of Marshall Matt Dillon on *Gunsmoke* only to turn it down and recommend his friend James Arness?

A290. What TV character had a white chess knight decorating his holster?

A291. Who wrote the music and lyrics to *Gigi*?

A292. Who worked for the fictionalized *Daily Bugle*?

ENTRY DEADLINE: September 12, 2000

A293. What was the original title of *Beverly Hills 90210*?

A294. What TV series was originally prepared as "The Linda Evans Project?"

A295. Whose performance in *The Bitch* won the actor a role in *Dynasty*?

A296. What group sings these lyrics:
> "She looked at me across the room,
> nudging from a silk cocoon
> lone beneath Venetian chandeliers.
> Against the moon her body rocks,
> her eyes were coming like a fox;
> wings of passion fly on all frontiers;
> from this body there's no returning,
> no escape, your heart is burning."

A297. In the 1960s, which folk group received two consecutive Grammy awards for Best Performance?

A298. Who wrote the song, "City of New Orleans?"

A299. In the 1980s, which male received three Grammies for Best Soul Gospel Performance?

A300. John Williams received a Grammy in 1975 for which film?

A301. Who sings these lyrics:
> "He comes for conversation;
> I comfort him sometimes.
> Comfort and consultation,
> He knows that's what he'll find."

A302. What two weapons did Starsky and Hutch use?

A303. What TV crime series was based upon the novel
  Poor, Poor Orphan?

A304. On *Bonanza*, Ben Cartwright had three marriages.
  What are the first names of these women and which
  sons did they give birth to?

A305. Who created *Beavis & Butt-Head?*

A306. For what TV series did a good proportion of audience males
  tune in to see Donna Douglas?

A307. In what year was the fictional bar, *Cheers*, established?

A308. Which two people created the TV show *Get Smart?*

A309. What fictional characters lived at 730 Hampton Street?

A310. What TV animated cartoon series was the first to appear as a
  Newsweek cover story?

A311. Which series, running from 1987 to 1991, featured an episode
  with two men in a bed—costing the network $1.5 million in lost
  advertising revenue?

A312. What film begins in an airport with a baggage handler cooking
  a hot dog in flames coming from a jet engine?

A313. In what film will you find either Clive or Scudder in intimate
  encounters with the title character?

A314. In what film does a 12-year-old refuse to play Little League ball
  because of nuclear weapons and rally the children of the world to
  support his efforts?

A315. What film portrays the adventures of Richard Burton and John Speke?

A316. In what film does a handicapped pianist marry an astrologer?

A317. In what film will you hear the following first line: "It was 1947, two years after the war, when I began my journey to what my father called the Sodom of the north—New York?"

A318. What 1970s film features the following dialogue:

"Has he asked for anything special?"

"Yes, this morning for breakfast he requested something called wheat germ, organic honey, and tiger's milk."

"Oh yes, those were the charmed substances that some years ago were felt to contain life preserving properties."

"You mean there was no deep fat, no steak or cream pies?"

"Those were thought to be unhealthy—precisely the opposite of what we now know to be true."

A319. In what film will you hear the following dialogue:

"Did you look in his citation book?"

"Yeah, the last vehicle he wrote in was a tan Sierra at 2:18 AM under a plate number—he put 'DLR'. I figure they stopped him or shot him before he could finish filling out the tag number."

PC1: Name this film that
takes place in the early 1900s.

PC2: Name this actor.

PC3: What is the name of this
producer and writer?

PC5: Who is this character?

PC4: Name this film.

PC6: What is the name of this special weapon?

PC8: Name this musician.

PC7: Name this actress and singer.

PC10: What is the name of this pro basketball player?

PC9: What is this impersonator called?

PC11: Who is this actor and writer?

PC12: What is the name of this California-based singer?

PC13: Who is this pro baseball player?

PC14: Who is this explorer?

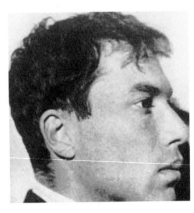

PC15: Who is this famous writer?

PC16: This actor is playing which ancient ruler?

B: ARTS & HUMANITIES

B1. What American won the first Tchaikovsky international competition in Moscow?

B2. Who composed the "Warsaw Concerto for Piano & Orchestra?"

B3. What does "BWV 1080" signify?

B4. How many Shakespeare plays feature ghosts with speaking roles?

B5. Who composed the "Easter Oratorio?"

B6. What is the name of the famous extract from Barber's "Quartet for Strings, Op. 11?"

B7. Which world famous artist worked for an international firm of picture dealers called Groupil & Company?

B8. What was the first published novel written on a typewriter?

B9. What James Joyce line provided the name for a sub-atomic particle?

B10. Who composed "Medea's Meditation and Dance of Vengeance?"

B11. Who composed the opera *Bluebeard's Castle*?

B12. What ancient dramatist supposedly died when an eagle dropped a turtle on his head?

B13. What novel portrays Professor Moriarty as having never actually been a criminal mastermind but in fact a mathematics genius?

B14. Which artist painted a work that could be called "moo moo with lemon-color countenance?"

B15. What is the second most translated book in the world after the Bible?

B16. Who composed the "Miraculous Mandarin?"

B17. Who composed "La damnation de Faust?"

B18. What poet, frustrated by an unrequited love affair, renounced all emotional preoccupations and dedicated himself to the "Idol of the Intellect?"

B19. Who performed the piano pieces stored on the two *Voyager* probes' information discs?

B20. In the King James Bible, what two books do not contain the word God?

B21. What two Sherlock Holmes stories have Sherlock as the narrator?

B22. What Athenian Cynic philosopher and advisor to Alexander the Great lived in a tub?

B23. Oscar Wilde said of what English artist and writer that he was neither flesh nor blood, but a "monstrous orchid?"

B24. From what specific ailment did Johannes Brahms die?

B25. Who called herself "Clematis" (Mental Beauty)?

B26. Who composed the "Harp Quartet?"

B27. Who composed the music for the opera "Lulu?"

B28. What are the "Chichester Psalms?"

B29. Fill in the blanks to name an orchestral work composed in 1880:

$$\_ \ C \ \_ \_ \_ \ E \ M \ \_ \_$$
$$\_ \ E \ \_ \ T \ I \ \_ \_ \ L$$
$$\_ \_ \ E \ R \ \_ \_ \ R \ \_$$

B30. What US novelist was named after the composer of "The Star Spangled Banner?"

B31. Who founded the *Sturm und Drang* movement?

B32. Who wrote a "Letter from Europe" series for the *Toronto Star*?

B33. In what novel will you find the Compson family?

B34. What novel is set in a land of live chessmen and talking insects?

B35. Who was Giuseppe Verdi's publisher?

B36. Who composed "Harold in Italy?"

B37. Who wrote the score for "On the Waterfront?"

B38. Which composer wrote a Hebrew rhapsody for cello and orchestra?

B39. What novelist had a 17-year affair with his student, Syed Ross Mosood, the grandson of a most influential Muslim in India?

B40. In what work does the writer denounce Christianity, while calling women the "most dangerous plaything?"

B41. In H.G. Wells' *The Time Machine*, in what year does the hero meet the Morlocks and Eloi?

B42. In what year was the opera *Les Troyens* composed?

B43. Who wrote an unfinished symphony in A minor in 1882?

B44. Which architect designed Baker House Dormitory at MIT?

B45. Who wrote *History of My Troubles* and *Dialogue Between a Philosopher, a Jew and a Christian*?

B46. Who wrote *De civitate Dei*?

B47. In 1758, who wrote the following?
> "Advertisements are now so numerous that they are very negligently perused, and it is therefore necessary to gain attention by magnificence of promise and by eloquence sometimes sublime and sometimes pathetick."

B48. Who is the Spanish-born Harvard naturalist who wrote about systematized aesthetics?

B49. Who wrote a play honoring Hieron's new city of Etna?

B50. What German critic and dramatist said: "We have actors but no art of acting?"

B51. In a famous play, what did Dr Stockmann discover?

Did You Know?

- You've seen statues of a person on a horse (the ones in parks and elsewhere); well if the horse has both front feet off the ground, then the rider died in battle. If the horse has one front leg in the air, the rider died as a result of wounds received in battle. If the horse has all four legs on the ground, then the person died of natural causes.

- US President Richard Nixon once said of Idi Amin, "He's a goddamn cannibal. A goddamn cannibal asshole. He'd eat his own mother. Christ! He'd eat his own grandmother!" (Source: *Cassell Dictionary of Insulting Quotations*.)

- In English, "four" is the only digit to have the same number of letters as its value.

B52. What Depression-era photographer produced *Elevator Garage* and *Girl With Leica*?

B53. What play by John Ford is set in Renaissance Italy and concerns incestuous love?

B54. What letters are assigned to the sources of the Hebrew Bible?

B55. Who is the famous poet with no capital letters in his name?

B56. Who was the leader of the Barbizon School?

B57. Who painted *The Mystical Marriage of St Catherine*?

B58. What Florentine artist was nicknamed "little barrel?"

 ENTRY DEADLINE: September 12, 2000

B59. What famous French painter was a prosperous banker who remained indifferent to his art until the final decade of his life?

B60. What is the name of the Boston, Massachusetts, artist who painted *The Boy with a Squirrel* in 1765?

B61. Who was appointed architect to the Florence Cathedral in 1334?

B62. What artist helped found the Phalanx, belonged to Berlin's Sezession, was a citizen of three countries, and created works from folk art to pure abstraction?

B63. Who painted *Inspiration of the Poet*?

B64. What artist became famous for drawing two-dimensional objects, such as flags, targets and numbers?

B65. *Perestroika* is the sub-title of what play?

B66. In what modern play does one character drag another "fortunate" character around by a leash and collar?

B67. Fill in the blanks to find out who lives in Oceania:

      _ I _ S T _ _   S _ I _ _

B68. Who wrote over 1,775 poems, and yet all but seven were published posthumously?

B69. Aeschylus and Shelly wrote works with which same word in the title?

B70. Who wrote *A la recherche du temps perdu*?

B71. What is the actual title that Daniel Defoe gave to the novel, *Robinson Crusoe*?

B72. "The Group of Seven" 20th Century artists had their headquarters in what North American city?

B73. Who painted *A Scene from the Beggar's Opera*?

B74. What is the name of the project undertaken during the FDR Administration to provide relief for unemployed artists?

B75. What was the first of Shakespeare's "Roman Plays?"

B76. The title character of which drama has a lover, Jean, who is her father's valet?

B77. In what novel does the hero attempt to write a biography of an 18th Century European politician but is overcome by a "sweetish sickness?"

B78. To what does "Ash-can School" refer?

B79. Which artist caused a sensation with his 1962 showing at New York's Castelli Gallery and has generally "Whaam?"-ed his followers ever since?

B80. Fill in the blanks to find a young artist:

　　　_ T _ P _ _ N　　　_ E _ A L _ S

B81. Who wrote *Essential Oils*?

B82. Who composed the "Funeral March" sonata for piano?

B83. Who is the protégé of Varvara Petrovna Stavrogina?

B84. Who suggested that the guardians of the ideal state should be educated as philosophers?

B85. *Rip Van Winkle* is based upon a folk tale from what country?

B86. Who coined the words "assassination" and "bump?"

B87. What two women served as the models for the Statue of Liberty?

B88. What was the first symphony to include trombones?

B89. Who was the first woman to conduct the Metropolitan Opera?

B90. For what "instrument" was *Imaginary Landscaper No. 4* composed?

B91. What is Mozart's full name?

B92. What Shakespeare character claims to be not only witty himself but the cause of wit in other men?

B93. What is the name of the Off Broadway play where the work takes place entirely in a 500 gallon aquarium?

B94. Who is the only author to have a book in every major Dewey Decimal category?

B95. Whose first three names are John Roland Reuel?

B96. What does the R. stand for in Dean R. Koontz?

B97. Who were Dismas and Gestas?

Did You Know?

- Since World War II, every US president to address the Canadian House of Commons in their first term of office has been re-elected to a second term. Eisenhower, Nixon, Reagan and Clinton all benefited from this, while Kennedy, Johnson, Ford, Carter and Bush missed the boat.

- The "walla-walla" scene in films is when extras pretend to be talking in the background but are actually saying "walla-walla."

- The *Addams Family* house was based upon College Hall at the University of Pennsylvania.

- The human body contains enough iron to make a spike strong enough to hold your weight.

B98. Who wrote the following?
"The point is this, she finally confided.
There has to be eternal chastisement.
That means eternal life. A bit one-sided,
All stick, no sugar. Listen, we're all sent
To see one big bedroom, Hitler undivided
From John the Twenty-Third, the innocent
And guilty raped and rapist, with no cup
Or tea or orange juice to wake us up."

B99. Who composed the "Choral Symphony?"

B100. Who wrote 21 "Hungarian Dances" for orchestra?

B101. In what comic play does the hero pose as his friend Jack's fictitious brother in order to court his friend's ward Cecily?

B102. What title character of a famous novel does not appear physically in the book for the first five hundred pages?

B103. Who authored a book about his escape from a WW II internment camp and traveled through Asia on foot with his friend Aufschnaiter?

B104. Fill in the blanks to name this "colossal" sculptor and graphic artist:

_ _ A _ S   _ _ _ E _ _ U _ _

B105. Who has won more National Book Awards for fiction than any other writer?

B106. Which book's subtitle is *JFK in the White House*?

B107. Of what literary genre is the book *Scrambled Eggs and Whiskey*?

B108. What is the only opera to receive a Pulitzer Prize for Music?

B109. For what two plays did Terrence McNally win consecutive Tony Awards?

B110. Which scholar's work relates Protestantism to capitalism and was greatly influenced by the ideas of Calvin?

B111. What title character obtains a job as assistant master at Dotheboys Hall, a wretched school for boys?

B112. What composer took 21 years to finish his first symphony (in C minor)?

B113. In what work will you hear the "Four Sea Interludes?"

B114. What is the "Seven Sonnets of Michelangelo?"

B115. To whom is the Newberry Medal awarded?

B116. Who wrote the "Kaddish Symphony?"

B117. What movement was inaugurated by Wertheimer, Kohler and Koffka?

B118. Who said that to attain beauty, pleasure must be disinterested, universal, necessary in a uniquely specified way, and must give the effect of purposiveness without being the satisfaction of a purpose?

B119. What is meant by "Deity E" and "Deity J?"

B120. What was George Tessman's special academic interest in *Hedda Gabler*?

B121. What is the complete name of the author Virgil?

B122. What ballet company celebrates its 227th anniversary in the year 2000?

B123. In what novel will you find the Abraham Licht family?

B124. What is the historical significance of Peri's *Dafne*?

B125. He was born in a hotel and spent his young years backstage watching his father act. He lived in Buenos Aires, Liverpool, and New York, and attempted suicide in his early 20s. Then he went on to win one of the world's most coveted awards. Who is he?

B126. Which opera by Monteverdi uses the text of Alessandro Striggio the Younger?

B127. In music, what is the quick reiteration of the same tone called?

B128. Who is known as the father of orchestration?

B129. In what novel will you find the characters Judge Thatcher and Joanna Wilks?

B130. Who are the only two lawgivers in the Old Testament?

B131. Written in Paris in the 18th Century, what famous theological study rails against institutional religion and the poison of atheism?

B132. In what work will you find the following characters: Subtle, Pertinax Surly, and Tribulation Wholesale?

B133. What Shakespeare character says, "Simply the thing I am shall make me live?"

B134. Which play was so successful with its audiences that the playwright received a generalship in the war against Samos?

B135. Who began his autobiography in Twyford, England, at the age of 65 and wrote about such key people in his life as Josiah, James, William Keith, and Mr Meredith?

B136. Who wrote about "Crazy Jane" and "Michael Robartes?"

B137. What character in a novel is attracted to a Polish boy named Tadzio?

Did You Know?

- Based upon market capitalization, each Ford Motor Company employee is valued at $143,000. Each AT&T employee is valued at $731,000. Each Microsoft employee is valued at $9 million. And the best for last, each Yahoo employee is valued at $13.7 million!

- According to a British law passed in 1845, attempting to commit suicide was a capital offense. Offenders could be hanged for trying.

- Comedienne Joan Rivers said of Bo Derek: "She turned down the role of Helen Keller because she couldn't remember the lines." (Source: Cassell Dictionary of Insulting Quotations.)

- On the same day he completed his masterpiece, *The Divine Comedy*, the Italian poet Dante died.

- Roger Ebert won the 1959 Illinois High School Association State Speech Competition and also wrote the screenplay for the film *Beyond The Valley Of The Dolls*.

- There is no single word given to describe the back of the knee.

B138. What collection of tales is set in 1348, the year of the Black Death?

B139. Who is Dante's guide during the last stage of his journey in *The Divine Comedy*?

B140. Who is Torvald Helmer?

B141. How many characters are there in the novel *Don Quixote de la Mancha*?

B142. In *Dracula*, Dr Van Helsing is a specialist from what city?

B143. Which guitar-playing Poe character attempts to bury his sister alive?

B144. In what novel will you find the characters Piani and Ettore Moretti?

B145. In what novel will you find the character Philip Pirrip?

B146. *For Whom the Bell Tolls* is an allusion to lines from what poem?

B147. In about 600 BC, what Indian text appeared that stressed mysticism and asceticism?

B148. In Hinduism, what is the "Godhead" called?

B149. E.M. Forster, Virginia Woolf, and John Maynard Keynes were members of what loosely knit organization?

B150. What 16th Century painter and draughtsman was often called the "Peasant?"

B151. What award do these people share in common: Clarence S. Stein, Eero Saarinen, and Romaldo Giurgola?

B152. Who illustrated the first edition of *A Study in Scarlet* by Arthur Conan Doyle?

B153. In what novel does Master Blifil bear false witness against the title character, his half-brother?

B154. Captain Smollett commands what ship on which Long John Silver is the cook?

B155. In what work will you find Sir Toby Belch?

B156. Which famous artist had an affair with Tommaso de' Cavalieri?

B157. Who was born on Bread Street, Cheapside, London in 1608?

B158. Who was Eric Arthur Blair?

B159. What is considered to be the world's first detective story?

B160. What famous child did this couple have: Harmen Gerritszoon van Rijn and Neeltgen Willems van Stuydtbrouck?

B161. What was Oscar Wilde's prison number?

B162. What famous author killed herself by filling her pockets with heavy stones and jumping into the river Ouse?

B163. After being named Poet Laureate, which English poet never wrote a line of poetry?

B164. Who composed the "Babi Yar" symphony?

B165. Who wrote "The Paradox of Acting" (1773-1778)?

B166. Who wrote the play in which all of the characters are in search of the Author?

B167. Who is the artist that produced 11 paintings of the Saint-Lazare station in Paris?

B168. Who wrote *Cigarrales de Toledo*?

B169. In Jainism, what is the term for any savior who transcends rebirths and makes a path for others to follow?

B170. Who composed a work for 13 percussion instruments in 1931?

B171. What books of the Bible are known as the Early Prophets?

B172. In what work will you find the character Chadwick Newsome?

B173. In what novel will you find these opening words:
"All happy families resemble one another, but each unhappy family is unhappy in its own way?"

B174. In what work will you find Taurus, Gallus, Agrippa and Menas?

B175. What Shakespeare play is based upon *Rosalyde* by Thomas Lodge?

B176. Which character's home was located in Floral Heights in the town of Zenith?

B177. Who wrote *Beowulf*?

B178. On what two ships did Billy Budd serve?

B179. Who wrote a play in which men and birds attempt to build a city together?

B180. Which poet wrote the following:
"All nature is but art, unknown to thee;
All chance, direction, which thou canst not see;
All discord, harmony not understood universe good:
And, in spite of pride, in erring reason's spite;
One truth is clear: whatever IS, IS RIGHT."

B181. In what Shakespeare play does the Battle of Agincourt occur?

Did You Know?

- On April 15, 1912, the SS Titanic sank on her maiden voyage and over 1,500 people died. Fourteen years earlier a novel was published by Morgan Robertson which seemed to foretell the disaster. The book described a ship the same size as the Titanic which crashes into an iceberg on its maiden voyage on a misty April night. The name of Robertson's fictional ship was Titan.

- Oscar Wilde once said "To disagree with three-fourths of the British public on all points is one of the first elements of sanity ..."

- Flying from London to New York by Concorde, due to the time zones crossed, you can arrive two hours before you leave.

- An alligator pear is an avocado.

- Since 1959, more than 6,000 pieces of 'space junk' (abandoned rocket and satellite parts) have fallen out of orbit. Many of these have hit the earth's surface.

B182. What epic poem is set during a three-day period in the Trojan War?

B183. What was Oscar Wilde's last play?

B184. What is the oldest of the world's great surviving religions?

B185. What is the family name of the three Middle Age Venetian painters whose first names are Jacopo, Gentile and Giovanni?

B186. What English poet, philosopher and artist prepared engravings for the Book of Job and The Divine Comedy?

B187. What two artists are credited with the creation of cubism?

B188. What Italian painter, named after his native town near Bergamo, produced homoerotic art in his early period?

B189. What famous artist illustrated a work by Gogol and designed costumes for Stravinsky's *Firebird*?

B190. Which Florentine painter is regarded as having founded the tradition of Western painting and is praised by Dante in *The Divine Comedy*?

B191. In what play will you find the title character saying, "This hash my life—this long disease my life?"

B192. Also a deacon, a lecturer in mathematics, and an accomplished photographer, who was this English writer who died in 1898?

B193. What two ships are there in *Twenty Thousand Leagues Under the Sea*?

B194. Which famous author's first wife was a cannibal?

B195. What author smoked 40 cigars a day and was called "Youth" by his wife?

B196. What author owned a 92-foot yacht named *Saint-Michel III*?

B197. Which writer and philosopher, who drank 50 cups of coffee each day, was known as "Zozo" as a child and as an adult was said to have the eloquence of Cicero, the elegance of Pliny, and the wisdom of Agrippa?

B198. What is the longest of Alexander Pushkin's complete prose tales?

B199. Which unfinished novel by Franz Kafka is sometimes referred to as a modern *Pilgrim's Progress*?

B200. Who wrote:

> "My thirteen books praise the righteous and good God as they speak either of my evil or good, and they are meant to excite men's minds and affections …?"

B201. In what novel will you find the line, "Barkis is willin'?"

B202. What is the English translation of *Et Dukkehjem*?

B203. What novel offers a history of the Salinas Valley and re-creates the Cain and Abel story?

B204. In what work will you find Sans Foy, Sans Loy and Sans Joy?

B205. In what Strindberg play is the captain driven to insanity by his wife and rejected by his own daughter?

B206. In Goethe's work, who is Faust's attendant?

B207. In the preface to his famous collection of poems, who advises: "Hypocrite reader—my likeness—my brother!"

B208. What novel has the subtitle: *Or, The Modern Prometheus?*"

B209. In which novel is the District Manager's only interest collecting ivory?

PC18: Name this actress.

PC17: Name this famous producer.

PC19: What film is this scene from?

PC20: Name this young actor.

PC21: Who is this
pro basketball player?

PC22: Who are these great thinkers?

PC23: What Western
Hemisphere city is this?.

PC24: This scene is from what film?

PC25: Name this 1960s pop group.

PC26: Who was this young woman?

PC27: Name this
pro basketball player.

PC28: What is the name of this famous
episode from the *I Love Lucy* show?

PC29: Name this
pro baseball player.

PC30: What is the name of this
oldest castle in Japan?

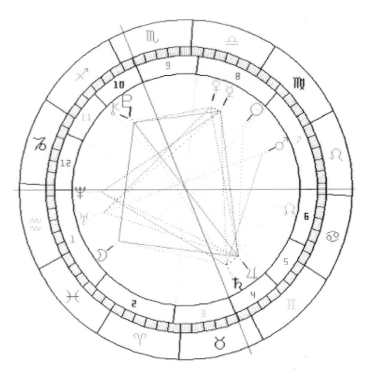

PC31: In this geocentric chart of the solar system, what "sign" is rising and
what two sets of outer planets are nearing conjunction?

C: TECHNOLOGY

Did You Know?

- The opposite sides of a dice cube always add up to seven.

- Every second, 4.2 babies are born and 1.7 people die. (On average, of course.)

- According to a 1995 UN study, Yemen had the highest fertility rate on earth, with each woman averaging 7.6 children per lifetime. Italy's rate was the lowest at 1.2.

- In Mel Brooks' film, *Blazing Saddles*, he portrays a governor called "Le Petomane," who is named after a French performer whose specialty was telling stories punctuated by flatulence.

- H. L. Mencken once said that "all government, in its essence, is a conspiracy against the superior man."

- Winds on the planet Neptune can reach velocities of 1500 miles per hour.

- In less than a 200-year period lived some of the world's greatest artists, such as Michelangelo, Raphael, Titian, El Greco, Velasquez, Rubens, da Vinci and Rembrandt.

C1. On what date was the first public radio broadcast?

C2. What is the AIM-54C Phoenix?

C3. What famous structure is a hyperbolic cosine?

C4. What are the two most common surgical operations in the USA?

C5. What was developed by deuteron bombardment of uranium-238 in a cyclotron?

C6. What was invented by John Augustus Larson in 1921?

C7. What is also known as polytetrafluoroethylene?

C8. What is the oldest man-made alloy?

C9. What glue is made by dissolving a milk product into an aqueous alkaline solvent?

C10. What do the Yak and the Zlín have in common?

C11. This natural abrasive is superior to flint and is used in the woodworking, leather and shoe industries. When its cutting edges break down, it fractures sharply and thus produces new cutting edges. What is this abrasive called?

C12. Who accomplished the first man-made nuclear reaction?

C13. From 1940 through 1945, the United States produced exactly how many military aircraft?

C14. What is the name of the system of crop farming where wheat is grown in the first year, followed by turnips in the second, then barley, with clover and ryegrass undersown, in the third; in the fourth year, clover and ryegrass is grazed or cut for feed?

C15. What's the name of a potential anti-obesity drug being developed by Amgen?

C16. Who manufactures Nextel phones?

C17. What lavender item is VAOI 505G?

C18. What's the name of the world's largest laser?

C19. What year was electricity first produced by atomic energy?

C20. What early weapon was made of a mixture of finely divided nitre, charcoal, and sulfur?

C21. What produces resolutions up to 500 times greater than an optical telescope?

C22. What is the name of the first space probe to soft land on Mars?

C23. What was the name of the first station in space in the 1970s?

C24. What animal did Luigi Galvani experiment on in 1791?

C25. Who was the first person to split the uranium atom?

C26. Who first described logarithms?

C27. Which two people independently discovered the calculus?

C28. How can a trillion be a billion?

C29. Who invented eyeglasses for nearsighted people?

C30. Who built the first navigable submarine?

C31. Which nation was first to use a fully electronic computer to crack enemy military codes?

C32. What was the "Harvard Mark I?"

C33. In what year was UNIVAC installed at the US Bureau of Census?

C34. Whose doctoral thesis was the first to describe the hypothetical "personal computer?"

C35. What company marketed the first hand-held mouse?

C36. Prodigy was launched by which two companies?

C37. In 1991, what company manufactured a computer capable of performing 9.03 billion calculations per second?

C38. In 1996, what produced $11.6 billion in revenue for the US telecommunications industry?

C39. Who created the World Wide Web (WWW)?

C40. Dust, dirt, soot, smoke and liquid droplets emitted into the air from factories, cars, and power plants are collectively known as what?

C41. What was the first man-made object to break the sound barrier?

C42. What does LASER stand for?

C43. What was known erroneously as "Montigolfier gas?"

C44. How long does it take radio signals from Earth to reach Pioneer 10?

C45. What was the first man-made object from Earth to leave the solar system?

C46. What provided the first evidence for the existence of black holes?

C47. What did the FDA approve on May 9, 1960?

C48. What two things were invented by William Powell Lear?

Did You Know?

- Of a person weighing 150 pounds, $97\frac{1}{2}$ pounds are oxygen.
- Mickey Mouse was originally called "Mortimer" after a real mouse that Walt Disney kept as a pet.
- The world's longest escalator is located in the St Petersburg Metro, and it's 120 meters long!
- US journalist Dan E. Moldea said of Jimmy Hoffa, "His most valuable contribution to the American labor movement came at the moment he stopped breathing on July 3, 1975."
- The Dutch town of Abcoude is the only reasonably sized town or city in the world whose name begins with ABC.
- All the dirt from the foundation to build the World Trade Center in New York City was dumped into the Hudson River to form the community now known as Battery Park City.

C49. Who owns the trademark for Unix?

C50. What was the first strike fighter to have a toilet in it?

C51. What product can be made from fresh slaughterhouse blood?

C52. The first flight with a turbojet engine occurred in what year?

C53. In information technology, what does A.D.S.L. stand for?

C54. What company is the 2nd largest manufacturer of telephone equipment in North America?

C55. What company manufactures PowerEdge Servers and Latitude Notebooks?

C56. Who manufactures the Optiplex Gxa 333 Desktop?

C57. What nation leads the world in the production of hydroelectric power?

C58. What European nation has the highest number of operable nuclear reactors?

C59. What and where is the world's largest optical telescope?

C60. The Hubble Space Telescope mirror is how many inches long?

C61. What is the name of the first space probe aimed at Mars?

C62. What does this equation solve for: $A = \frac{1}{2} bh$?

C63. What is a 1 followed by a googol of zeroes?

C64. What people first developed concrete?

C65. In what country was the first known gun made?

C66. Who was the person to patent margarine?

C67. What is "pascaline?"

C68. ENIAC was designed by which two men?

C69. What company introduced the first word processor?

C70. What was the MITS Altair 8800?

Did You Know?

- A group of unicorns is called a blessing. Twelve or more cows are known as a flink. A group of frogs is called an army. A group of rhinos, a crash. A group of kangaroos is called a mob, a group of whales, a pod; a group of geese, a gaggle; a group of ravens, a murder; a group of owls is called a parliament.

- If you could remove all the space between the atoms that make up your body, you could walk through the eye of a needle.

- President Lyndon B. Johnson once said of J. Edgar Hoover, "I'd rather have him inside the tent pissing out, than outside, pissing in." (Source: *Cassell Dictionary of Insulting Quotations.*)

- "Dios Mio! There's an OVNI in the sky!"

- In Kansas City, a federal agency ordered a bank to put a Braille keypad on a drive-through ATM.

- More money is spent each year on alcohol and cigarettes than on life insurance.

- The first significant genocide of the 20th Century began in 1915 against Armenians by the Turks, who slaughtered 800,000 to two million people.

- John Quincy Adams called Thomas Jefferson "a slur upon the moral government of the world." (Source: *Cassell Dictionary of Insulting Quotations.*)

- The giraffe has an 18-inch tongue.

C71. In 1997, what sold more units in the USA: cellular phones, home computers, fax and/or modems, telephone answering machines, or cordless telephones?

C72. What is the world's largest communications network?

C73. In environmental terms, what is MSW?

C74. Who invented the transistor?

C75. What was "CDC 1604?"

C76. What was the first commercial computer to use a keyboard and monitor instead of punched cards?

C77. What computer was the first to use magnetic disks for storage?

C78. What computer was the first to predict a presidential election victory?

C79. In whose garage was Apple Computer founded?

C80. What was the model and nickname of the IBM machine that beat a world chess champion?

C81. What was the name of the first chip to contain one million transistors?

C82. What company released the first laptop computer with VGA display?

C83. According to the Bible, who reigned in 8th Century BC and made " ... engines to shoot arrows and great stones?"

C84. What was "WordStar" and which company released it?

C85. In what year was MS-DOS released?

C86. What was the list price of Apple's first Macintosh computer released in 1984?

C87. What computer, released in 1985, was capable of 1.2 billion operations per second?

C88. *Softbook* and *Rocketbook* are examples of what new type of media released in late 1998?

C89. What is the *Armada 1700*?

C90. What is the maximum Kbps that an ISDN connection provides?

C91. What is WinWord.CAP?

C92. Fill in the blanks to find the name of a 7-CD-ROM journey to the paranormal:

_ - _ I _ E _   _ A _ _

C93. What manufacturer produces a model 740il?

C94. Fill in the blanks to the possible heir-apparent to HTML:

_ _ T _ N _ I _ _ E   _ _ R _ _ P
_ _ N _ _ A G _

C95. What company first introduced videophones in 1964?

C96. In the late 19th Century, how did nitroglycerin improve weapons systems?

C97. What country used rocket-firing jet fighters called Me 262s?

C98. On a modern Chinese abacus, what is the highest number bar?

C99. Weighing about six tons, the A-bomb dropped on Hiroshima contained how many pounds of Uranium-235?

C100. Who made the first officially observed airplane flight in Europe?

C101. What was the first cable-wire steel suspension bridge in the world?

C102. In what year was the first telephone cable completed across the Atlantic Ocean?

C103. What art form and technology's name is derived from the Greek, meaning "drawing by light?"

C104. What university has a nuclear research center in Saxonburg, Pennsylvania?

C105. By US industry standards, how many pounds are there in a bag of cement?

C106. What was the name of the first locomotive engine to use smooth wheels on smooth tracks?

C107. What organization designates the film speed of a camera?

C108. The name of what science is derived from the Greek word *tribein*, meaning to rub?

C109. Similar to the American Gatling gun developed in the 1860s, what was the name of the French machine gun that delivered 370 rounds per minute?

C110. What is the name of the computer memory storage system that consists of a thin chip of synthetic garnet with tiny, magnetic domains?

C111. In metallurgy, what is the term for useless materials, such as sand, dirt and rock?

C112. What scientific instrument uses backscattered and secondary electrons?

C113. What is the "Geneva pulldown movement?"

C114. What are the four methods of navigation at sea?

C115. What type of atomic reactor uses either carbon dioxide or helium as the coolant?

C116. What was the full name of the observatory launched into space in 1978 to study X-rays?

C117. What is the name of the process of pulp production that utilizes sodium hydroxide and sodium sulfide in the cooking liquor?

C118. What common product is made of surface-active agents?

C119. What is the name of the US-Canada jointly operated radar network to monitor artificial satellites?

C120. Fill in the blanks to discover what are known as reciprocating devices:

_ I _ _ O _ - _ _ L I _ _ E _   _ _ M _ S

C121. What term is applied to all processes and physical measurements carried out under conditions of below-normal atmospheric pressure?

PC32: What is this fictional
object called?

PC33: Name this early pop group.

PC34: Who is this writer?

PC35: Who is this economist?

PC36: What is the name of this lake and where is it found?

PC37: What's the name of this early
TV celebrity's show?

PC38: This scene is from what film?.

PC39: Who was this thinker
and mathematician?

PC40: Name this
pro baseball player.

PC41: Who is the sculptor
and what is the subject?

PC42: Name the cartoonist.

PC43: In what North American city
will you find this location?

PC44: Who is this
pro basketball player?

PC45: Name this model.

ENTRY DEADLINE: September 12, 2000

D: THE SCIENCES

Astronomy
Physics
Chemistry
Biology
Medicine

Did You Know?

- Well over 50 million Americans own guns.

- The mad emperor Caligula once decided to go to war with the Roman God of the Sea, Poseidon, and thus he ordered his soldiers to throw their spears into the water at random.

- Some Eskimos have been known to use refrigerators to keep their food from freezing.

- The percentage of high school seniors with an A average who smoke cigarettes daily is 7%. The percentage of seniors with a D average who smoke daily is 46%.

- No piece of paper can be folded in half more than 7 times.

- The sound of *E.T.* walking was made by someone squishing her hands in Jello.

- Every bird and mammal except the spiny anteater experiences REM (rapid eye movement) during sleep.

- Bigamy is having one husband too many. Monogamy is the same.

D1. What do you call an airborne group of geese?

D2. What is the only letter that does not appear in the Periodic Table of Elements?

D3. What is calcium sulphate hemihydrate more commonly known as?

D4. What is a circumorbital hematoma?

D5. In what country do the smallest trees in the world grow?

D6. What is the significance of "gp120?"

D7. The Sun is how many light years away from the center of the galaxy?

D8. Where will you find the "Equal House" system used?

D9. How many knots signify a strong gale?

D10. What communicable disease is the leading cause of death worldwide?

D11. What work published in the 19th Century convinced geologists that the Earth was at least several hundred million years old?

D12. In what Era did the dinosaurs emerge?

D13. What are the two oldest surviving organisms on earth?

D14. Who discovered that water is composed of hydrogen and oxygen?

D15. Who is known as the father of entropy?

D16. Humans belong to what Superfamily?

D17. What was discovered in the Olduvai Gorge of northern Tanzania in 1961?

D18. In Kelvin degrees, what is the average human body temperature?

D19. What is the largest Satellite Galaxy in the Milky Way?

D20. How many miles per second does the Sun move in its orbit?

D21. What are the two largest galaxies in the Local Group?

D22. Fill in the blanks to discover who published the first map ever
made of the Milky Way's structure:

_ _ _ L _ A _   _ _ R _ C _ _ L

D23. Fill in the blanks to find the name of doughnut-shaped belts:

_ _ _   _ _ L _ N
_ _ D _ A _ _ _ N   _ _ _ _ _ S

D24. What is the color from a wavelength of 6563 Angstroms?

D25. Who coined the astronomical term "subdwarfs?"

D26. Atomic hydrogen emits what kind of radio waves?

D27. WIMPs and MACHOs are used to theorize about what part
of the Galaxy?

D28. According to the Big Bang theory, what was the first step in the
creation of elements in the early universe?

D29. "A0620-00" is thought to be what?

D30. About 100,000 molecules of ozone can be destroyed by just one
atom of what element?

D31. In what nation will you find the endangered species,
the silvery gibbon?

D32. Whose first published work was a monograph on barnacles?

D33. In Feynman's "theory of sum over histories," a particle in space-
time can travel how many paths?

D34. What is the total energy of the universe?

D35. What does the Einstein-Rosen bridge connect?

D36. What theory describes the interactions of quarks and gluons?

D37. What species is also known by a shorter name than
Australopithecus afarensis?

D38. What species is also known as the "Handyman?"

D39. The name of what part of the body is derived from the Greek,
meaning "air duct?"

D40. In biology, what is the *milieu intérieur?*

D41. Bergson proposed what type of hypothetical energy?

D42. The peripheral nervous system comprise what two sub-systems?

D43. What part of the neuron branches like a tree?

D44. What is the general term for molecules that excite or
inhibit neurons?

D45. Fill in the blanks to discover what muscle protects the testicles
from injury:

_ A _ _ _ S

D46. What is the name of the master regulatory genes that lay out the
general geographic plan of the human body?

D47. About 30% of the genes in the human body code for what organ?

Did You Know?

- The octopus' testes are located in its head.

- Glass is actually a liquid; over time, it will "ooze" down due to gravity's pull. Look at the windows in very old (Colonial) buildings—it will be thicker at the bottom of the pane.

- Hitler was a vegetarian.

- A boy gave General Rahl of the British Army a note from a spy saying George Washington was about to cross the Delaware and attack. The general was so immersed in a chess game that he put the note in his pocket unopened. There it was found when he was mortally wounded in the subsequent battle.

- Non-dairy creamer is flammable.

- Long distance telephone calls over the Internet are as low as 4.9 cents a minute, as of 1998.

- The average teacher spent more than $400 from his or her own pocket for classroom materials in 1994-1995.

- John Adams said of George Washington, "He is too illiterate, unread, unlearned for his station and reputation." (Source: *Cassell Dictionary of Insulting Quotations*.)

D48. What part of the brain distinguishes humankind from animal?

D49. What lobe of the brain governs smell?

D50. What writer proclaims that evolution is an algorithmic process built by cranes and not by skyhooks?

D51. What is "Jacobson's Organ?"

D52. What is the only animal besides humans that can contract leprosy?

D53. What is the only bird that can see the color blue?

D54. What is an elver?

D55. What is the white part of the fingernail called?

D56. What is the only mammal that has hair on the soles of its feet?

D57. How many phalanges does the normal human have?

D58. What fleshy muscular organ is joined to the hyoid bone?

D59. How is the "Babinsky Effect" produced?

D60. What are a rabbit's dowsets?

D61. In astronomy, taken collectively, what do the following measure: U, V, & W?

D62. What was the first heart medicine discovered in 1799?

D63. What is the only part of the human body that cannot repair itself?

D64. What is the world's smallest mammal?

D65. In the cat family, what is the *tapetum lucidum*?

D66. 900 grit equal how many inches?

D67. How many electron volts are in 1 GeV?

D68. What is the key element in acids?

D69. What are names of the two processes in stars that produce heavy elements?

D70. In what part of the Galaxy will you find *Kapteyn's Star*?

D71. Planetary nebulae eject what two heavy elements into the Galaxy?

D72. Iron is produced by what type of supernova?

D73. Where is *Sagittarius A**?

D74. What Satellite Galaxy is moving fastest toward the Galactic center?

D75. What kind of species is the *Moapa coriacea*?

D76. Each "flavor" of a quark comes in which three colors?

D77. The concept of entropy explains which "arrow of time?"

D78. The name of what part of the body is derived from the Greek word, *karotikos*?

D79. Fill in the blanks to find out where the great majority of cancer cells are killed within the body:

$$\_ \_ \_ O \_ \_ T R \_ A \_$$

D80. What chemical enables the crossing of the open junction between a nerve ending and the muscle it activates?

D81. Governed by centers in the hypothalamus, which part of the nervous system responds to sudden dangerous or exhilarating stimuli?

D82. T4 and CD4 cells are destroyed by what virus?

D83. What is the name of the syndrome that is characterized by the sudden onset of a multiplicity of scars on the skin, excruciating stomach pain, bleeding from the lungs, and/or convulsions?

D84. Who synthesized LSD in 1938?

D85. What animal was originally called the Camelopard?

D86. What do you get when you cross a yak with a cow?

D87. What animal lays the largest eggs?

D88. What metal is the best conductor of electricity?

D89. What is the only animal that can see both ultraviolet and infrared light?

D90. How is fulgurite formed?

D91. What are the only kind of rocks found in the ice of Antarctica?

D92. What caused Niagara Falls to practically dry up in 1848?

D93. What are Alaska's two monotremes?

D94. What seven moons of the solar system are larger than the planet Pluto?

D95. Which fingernail grows the quickest?

D96. How many Earth hours is a Uranus day?

D97. Which animal is responsible for the extinction of the dodo bird?

D98. What is a pregnant goldfish called?

D99. From its ocean base to its summit, what mountain is actually higher than Mt Everest?

D100. What is the only marsupial with a pouch on its back?

D101. What is the smallest unit of time?

D102. What do you get when you cross a male horse with a female donkey?

D103. What teleost native to the Ganges River is commonly studied by molecular biologists because of its fast-developing embryos?

D104. In cubic centimeters, what is the approximate volume of an adult brain?

D105. In what building will you find "The Hall of Biodiversity?"

D106. What is the name of the 15 consecutive elements in the Periodic Table whose significance is their radioactivity?

D107. How many decibels are generated by a whisper?

D108. In aeronautics, what does L/D stand for?

D109. How many miles are in a light year?

D110. What is the name of this ion: H+ ?

D111. The neutrino was discovered by scientists at what laboratory?

D112. Within 10,000, how many people die each year in America because of excess weight?

D113. White dwarf stars make up what percent of the stars in the Galaxy?

D114. Who published a three-volume catalog containing the positions and magnitudes of 454,875 stars?

D115. Who discovered that the Milky Way rotates?

D116. Who discovered the electron?

D117. What is O B A F G K M?

D118. What "arm" of the Galaxy contains the Sun?

D119. What radio wave "broadcasts" at 21 centimeters?

D120. B^2FH refers to what four authors?

D121. What Satellite Galaxy is moving fastest away from the Galactic center?

D122. How many neutrons does Hydrogen-I have?

D123. What are "IRS 7" and "IRS 16?"

D124. Of the Sun's nearest neighbors, which one has the highest apparent visual magnitude?

D125. In 1773, William Herschel discovered that the solar system was moving toward what constellation?

Did You Know?

- 80% of all wounds inflicted during the Civil War were in the extremities.
- In the 1970s, the Rhode Island Legislature entertained a proposal to place a $2.00 tax on every act of sexual intercourse in the state.
- When Albert Einstein died, his final words died with him. The nurse at his side did not understand German.
- Iceland is the world's oldest functioning democracy.
- For Roman Catholics, January 5th is St Simeon Stylites' Day. He was a 5th Century hermit who showed his devotion to God by spending years sitting on top of a huge flagpole.
- The man who wrote the original M*A*S*H novel, Richard Hornberger, refused to watch the TV series because he was a conservative Republican and the program was too liberal for him.
- In 1911, three men were hung for the murder of Sir Edmund Berry at Greenbury Hill, and their last names were Green, Berry, and Hill.

D126. What planet's atmosphere is virtually all helium?

D127. The name of which constellation means "furnace?"

D128. In what Epoch did *Homo erectus* emerge?

D129. Who discovered the Periodic Table of Elements?

D130. Who discovered ultraviolet rays?

D131. In the equation, $E = hf$, what does "h" stand for?

D132. Who first observed bacteria?

D133. In what specific area of the world will you find the giant Kangaroo rat?

D134. What do particles of spin $1/2$ comprise?

D135. What does the cosmological constant allow space to do?

D136. What does "cognitive closure" mean?

D137. What part of the brain responds when blood pressure drops?

D138. When is GnRH released?

D139. About 90% of blood plasma consists of what?

D140. What body cells are the "big eaters?"

D141. Fill in the blanks to find out what mediates our emotions and instincts:

_ I _ _ I _   _ _ _ T _ M

D142. What animal has the longest sperm ever recorded?

D143. What are dinosaur droppings called?

D144. What is the most abundant mineral on earth?

D145. What is the most southern constellation in the zodiac?

D146. What is the Sun's nearest star?

Did You Know?

- The Mayflower, the ship that crossed the Atlantic in 1620 with 102 colonists, still exists — sort of. After the ship returned to England from its historic voyage, it was purchased in 1624 by a farmer named Russel, who floated the Mayflower up the Thames River to his farm. He disassembled the ship and used the timbers to build a barn that still stands today in Old Jordans, Bucks, UK. William Penn asked to be buried next to the old barn when he died in England in 1726.

- On average, Americans throw away 20,000 televisions, 150,000 tons of packaging materials, and 43,000 tons of food per day.

- One human brain generates more electrical impulses in a single day than all of the world's telephones put together.

- Mongooses were brought to Hawaii to kill rats. This ingenious plan failed because rats are nocturnal, while the mongoose hunts during the day and sleeps at night.

- Both Hitler and Napoleon were missing one testicle.

D147. Red dwarf stars make up what percentage of all the stars in the Galaxy?

D148. What star, first discovered in 1784, pulsates every 7.176779 days?

D149. What yellow supergiant stars serve as one tool to measure astronomical distances?

D150. What are the common names of the M33 and M51 galaxies?

D151. What part of the brain accounts for 85% of its weight?

D152. Fill out the blanks to find out where left meets right:

__ R P __   _ A _ _ O _ _ _

D153. When activity in the reticular formation decreases, what is induced?

D154. What chemical in the sperm's tail provides energy for lashing movements?

D155. Channels draining the gut of digested fat are part of what major body system?

D156. Whose theory stated that any moderately complex system of axioms inevitably raises questions that cannot be answered by the axioms?

D157. Who originally proposed the "Gaia" concept?

D158. Who proposes the computational theory of the mind and has said: "The ultimate goal that the mind was designed to attain is maximizing the number of copies of the genes that created it?"

D159. What do massive vector bosons carry?

D160. What idea attempts to explain why there is so much matter in the universe?

D161. What is a "naked singularity?"

D162. What medical term is taken from the Greek, meaning "a move from one place to another?"

D163. Collectively, what do these refer to: Sa, Sb, and Sc?

D164. Having never taken any courses in astronomy, who was the first person to link the luminosities and colors of stars?

D165. What "arm" of the Galaxy is closest to the Galactic center?

D166. What are the two most distant galaxies in the Galactic empire?

D167. Who first detected radio waves?

D168. What is the name of the constant used to measure the age of the universe?

D169. One megaparsec is how many light years?

D170. Of the Ross stars 128, 154, and 248, which is closest to Earth?

D171. Stephen Hawking is a proponent of the Big Bang Theory. True or False?

D172. What two moons in the solar system are named after Roman mythical horses, "terror" and "fear?"

D173. What geological formation in the solar system is about three times the height of Mt Everest?

D174. What are the three largest families of flowering plants?

D175. Where will you find "Maxwell Montes?"

D176. The name of which constellation means "harp?"

D177. The melting point of which element is 2,444 degrees F?

PC46: Name this actor.

PC47: Name this
19th Century thinker.

PC48: This scene is from what film?

PC49: Name the city where
you will find this building.

PC50: What is the year
and make of this car?

PC51: Name this
pro baseball pitcher.

PC52: In what film
does this scene appear?

PC53: The FBI consifcated these
weapons from what crime group?

PC54: Name this actor.

Jackie Chan

PC55: Which midwestern university has this logo?

PC56: Name this influential 20th Century philosopher.

PC57: In what TV series will you find this symbol?

PC58: Name this actress.

PC59: What is the name of this 1970s and 1980s soul and R&B group?

E: HISTORY & POLITICS

E1. What is the name of the "water czar" who opened the Los Angeles Aqueduct in 1913?

E2. How many people were killed when a US Marine jet sliced a gondola cable in the Italian Alps?

E3. Who is the leader of the Montana Freemen?

E4. What religious group, citing the "Epistle to the Ephesians," re-affirmed that the submission of wives to their husbands is "clearly revealed in Scripture?"

E5. In what year did the first automobile accident occur?

E6. What was the first city in the United States to add fluoride to its tap water to help prevent cavities?

E7. What Pope was formerly a sergeant in the Italian army?

E8. Who was the only British king to be crowned on the battlefield?

E9. What was Dr W. S. Halstead first to use in 1890?

E10. Who was imprisoned for doing the horoscope of Jesus Christ?

E11. Who are the only married couple to have gone to space together?

E12. What kind of gun killed Lincoln?

E13. Which US president had a pet alligator?

E14. What is the world's oldest functioning democracy?

E15. What did Ben Franklin suggest should be the national bird?

E16. Who was the consul and co-regent of Rome under Caligula from 37-41 AD?

E17. Who is the only left-handed president to serve two terms?

E18. Who was the first US president to have been born in a hospital?

E19. Who was the last astronaut to fly in space alone in a spacecraft?

E20. Who signed the Declaration of Independence on July 4th, 1776?

E21. According to Al Capone's business card, what business was he in?

E22. Who is Meles Zenawi?

E23. What is the name of the mayor of Teheran who was put on trial for embezzlement?

E24. In 1998, what company settled a sexual harassment lawsuit filed by the US Federal Government for $34 million?

E25. What US Congressman said: "Cyberpredators often cruise the Internet in search of lonely, curious or trusting young people?"

E26. What organization was embarrassed by its product endorsement deal with Sunbeam Corporation?

E27. What famous journalist and editor died at the age of 67, June 10, 1998, in St Thomas' Hospital?

E28. In what years were the Eisenhower dollars minted?

E29. Until the 1860s, which country was the main source of diamonds?

E30. Who relinquished his chancellorship to Ludwig Erhard?

E31. In what city was the world's first organized adult education school located?

E32. Reynell & Son was founded in 1812 to perform what service?

E33. Fill in the blanks and come up with a prominent political world figure.

_ A _ I _   A _ I _

E34. What reverberating events occurred in the world on May 11 and May 13, 1998?

E35. Who assassinated Yitzhak Rabin?

E36. In what country will you find the "One Nation" political party?

E37. In 1994, what country hosted an ad hoc war crimes tribunal to try people taking part in the genocide in Rwanda?

E38. Why has the US Federal Government decided to give each of 1200 Latin Americans of Japanese descent a payment of $5000.00?

E39. In what city did the 1995 peace accords occur, which ended nearly four years of fighting in Bosnia?

E40. What do these people have in common: Olusegun Obasanjo, Beko Ransome-Kuti, Frank Kokori, and Milton Dabibi?

E41. What US politician voted against a bill to ban discrimination against homosexuals in the work place and yet said of any homosexual, "You still love that person and you should try not to mistreat them or treat them as outcasts."

E42. What was the "Hollywood 10?"

E43. What were the years of Mao's Cultural Revolution?

E44. What political office building was demolished in Ho Chi Minh City in June 1998?

E45. What is the name of the Islamic movement in Afghanistan which closed 100 girls' schools to keep women out of public life?

E46. What war led to the tolerance of Protestant & Catholic missionaries in China?

E47. Who is Kipland P. Kinkel?

E48. What California county went bankrupt in 1994?

E49. Whose nomination for a US ambassadorship to Luxembourg was held up because of his homosexuallity?

E50. In what magazine's first issue did the article "Pressgate" appear?

E51. Who were recruited by the CIA in Laos for covert military actions in the Vietnam War?

E52. Who was John Graves Simcoe?

E53. Who put salmonella in the sugar at an African National Congress convention?

Did You Know?

- In 1963, baseball pitcher Gaylord Perry remarked, "They'll put a man on the moon before I hit a home run." On July 20, 1969, a few hours after Neil Armstrong set foot on the moon, Gaylord Perry hit his first and only home run.

- Scientists found a whole new phylum of animal on a lobster's lip

- Lichtenstein was a "Whammer."

- During the chariot scene in *Ben Hur*, a small red car can be seen in the distance.

- The British Parliament proceedings are supposed to be private—even though they are televised. So, if the MPs want to have a secret session, one of them points to the gallery from which the public watch and calls, "I spy strangers!" Then the MPs vote "that the strangers do withdraw."

- Each year ten new stars are born in the Milky Way galaxy.

- A baseball thrown at 30 miles per hour can cause sudden death from heart failure if it strikes the chest at precisely the wrong moment in the heartbeat cycle.

E54. The Peloponnesian War was recorded by what Greek historian?

E55. Who sacked Rome in 410 AD?

E56. What was the *Great Schism*?

E57. In the 15th Century, which two countries in a treaty divided the world by a line 370 leagues west of the Azores?

E58. Whose slogan was: "Land to the tiller?"

E59. How many times did the Roman Empire have co-emperors?

E60. Henry IV was king of which dynasty from 1589-1610?

E61. Who was the first Pope?

E62. In what year was Siddhartha Gautama (Buddha) born?

E63. What important 16th Century political treatise begins with a discussion of the kinds of principalities and the means by which they are acquired?

E64. Pashtun, Tajik, Hazara, and Uzbek comprise the ethnic groups of what Asian country?

E65. Which nation gained its independence from the federation of UK colonies on January 1, 1901?

E66. What former World Bank official was named prime minister of an African nation in 1990?

E67. Which explorer first reached the beaches of Brazil in 1500?

E68. Who was the first secretary of the Bulgarian Communist Party?

E69. In what year was the first permanent European settlement established in Canada?

E70. What countries fought the Ten Years War from 1868-1878?

E71. Which nation's troops liberated Denmark in May 1945?

E72. What African nation was formerly called Territory of the Afars and Issas?

E73. What was the only nation to register zero births in 1983?

E74. Who was the first US president to win the Nobel Peace Prize and for what did he win it?

E75. Who was the youngest US general?

E76. What cost the British $72,414 in 1509?

E77. In U.S. dollars and cents, how much did Freud pay per gram for his first sample of cocaine?

E78. What did Harold Edgerton photograph?

E79. What was the shortest war on record?

E80. Who was Iosif Djugashvili?

E81. What nations joined NATO in 1951?

E82. In 1995, which national President received a 99.96% vote of approval for another term in office?

E83. What nation has a bicameral legislature consisting of a 315-member Senate and a 630-member Chamber of Deputies?

E84. What nation is home to the Secretariat of the European Parliament and the European Investment Bank?

E85. What nation celebrates the national holiday, Queen's Day, on April 30th?

E86. Which organization launched a CyberSchoolBus to reach children worldwide?

E87. What extremely significant astronomical event occurred on April 24, 1990?

E88. What volcano's eruptions were attributed to causing 162,000 deaths?

E89. How much money did Alfred Nobel bequest for the Nobel prizes?

E90. Who founded the Lambarene Hospital?

E91. What famous philosopher was found guilty of 23 counts of corruption, fined £40,000 and briefly imprisoned in the Tower of London?

E92. What city hosted the 1998 annual meeting of the American College of Sports Medicine?

E93. What nation was first settled by Maori voyagers from Polynesia in the 9th Century?

E94. In what capacity did Lisa Schiffren serve Vice President Dan Quayle?

E95. What medal dated 1796 alludes to a proposed French settlement in Carthage, New York?

E96. His younger brother was named Brooks. His older brother was named Charles Francis Jr. He graduated from Harvard in 1858. His father was minister to England. Who was he?

Did You Know?

- $600,000 is the size of the fine levied by the FCC on Howard Stern's employer for his discussion of masturbation, erections, and homosexual sex during his show. $10,000 was the size of the fine issued to Charles Barkley by the NBA for accidentally spitting on an eight year old girl. $7,500 was the size of the fine issued by the French Open to John McEnroe for swearing during his loss in the tournament's first round. $1,000 was the fine issued by the State of Texas to a man arrested for possession of four automatic weapons and five silencers.

- If heart disease, cancer, and diabetes were eliminated, the life expectancy for both men and women would leap to 100 years.

- In Hitchcock's film *North by Northwest*, during the scene with the gunshot towards the end, in the background a young boy puts his finger in his ears because he knew what was coming up because of lots of retakes.

- By the year 2002, it is estimated that 18 million brokerage accounts will be on the Internet, with $880 billion in assets.

E97. What is the name of the civilization from about 3000 to 1000 BC that included Crete, the Greek mainland, and Thessaly?

E98. As of 1997, how many Nobel Peace Prizes were not awarded to individuals?

E99. In 1998, what world leader ordered his country's military forces to relinquish their multi-billion dollar commercial enterprises to regain their purity?

E100. How many judges sit on the World Court (International Court of Justice)?

E101. What four US presidents have served an entire term without a vice president?

E102. Which Iranian minister said, "Muslims now feel more confident that Pakistan's nuclear capacity would play a role of deterrence to Israel's?"

E103. In what year did the Qing Dynasty end?

E104. What US Congressman cited I Corinthians 6:9, 11, 18 & 20 to bolster his claim that homosexuality is a sin?

E105. What company established Ft Vancouver in 1824?

E106. What is the name of the first Russian to fly on a US Space Shuttle mission?

E107. What nation captured and pillaged what is now called Toronto in the 19th Century?

E108. About a thousand years before Christ, the Kingdom of Israel flourished under what three kings?

E109. What city emerged in 716 BC?

E110. Fill in the blanks to discover a depressing historical location:
       _ U _ _ H _ I _ _

E111. Which group chopped off the left foot and right hand of a convicted robber in a sports stadium in Afghanistan?

E112. What nation has a 282-seat bicameral parliament?

E113. Where did Christopher Columbus land on October 12, 1492?

Did You Know?

- Robert G. Ingersoll once said, "No man with a sense of humor ever founded a religion."

- In 1979 Dr. Christian Barnard was offered $250,000 by the *National Enquirer* to perform a human head transplant.

- Thomas A. Edison was taught by his mother after schools were unsuccessful at the task.

- If college costs continue their present 6% annual upward climb, a freshman in 2012 could need $112,250 to $235,000 to cover four years of college.

- Assuming Rudolph is in front, there are 40,320 ways to arrange the other eight reindeer.

E114. What nation gained its independence from Pakistan in December 1971?

E115. Who was the son of King Philip (356-330 BC)?

E116. Who was the first human to orbit the earth 17 times?

E117. What is located at 7, Place de Fontenoy, 75007, Paris, France?

E118. Fill in the blanks to find the name of this very prominent, worldwide figure:

_ O _ I   _ _ N _ _

E119. Jesus was born under what Roman emperor and died under what Roman emperor?

E120. What did Canada's "equalization payments" seek to accomplish?

E121. What nation celebrates its National Day on October 1st?

E122. What country received its independence from Spain on November 9, 1949?

E123. What did Quebec, Ontario, Nova Scotia and New Brunswick accomplish in 1867?

E124. The first Chinese Empire was under what dynasty?

E125. By the year 1000, what were the four major centers of civilization?

E126. Between 1815 and 1855, one million Britons emigrated to what country?

E127. What northern European country celebrates its national holiday on December 6th?

E128. The EPLF established what nation in 1983?

E129. What emperor's personal emblem was a bee?

E130. Fill in the blanks to find the name of a ruthless Jewish gangster:
_ _ E   _ _ L _ S

E131. Who was known as "The Lady of the Lamp?"

E132. Whose last words were: "What an artist the world is losing in me?"

E133. Who was Akhenaton's son-in-law?

E134. In the 18th Century, who were the first victims of the *Reign of Terror?*

E135. Who were the first two French explorers to reach America in the 16th Century?

E136. In what year did England separate itself from the Catholic Church?

E137. How many member nations serve on the UN Security Council?

E138. Fill in the blanks to discover the name of a former world political figure who was accused of human rights abuses during his tenure:

$$\_ \cdot \_ \cdot \quad \_ O T \_ \_$$

E139. What school teacher was killed in the Space Shuttle explosion?

E140. In what year did Europe begin nearly 100 years of peace?

E141. In what year did Germany emerge as the Weimar Republic?

E142. In 1956, 1968, and 1981, what countries held anti-Soviet uprisings?

E143. Who was the first king of England?

E144. In what year did the Holy Roman Empire begin?

E145. What is the previous name of the House of Windsor?

E146. What nation will be changing G-7 to G-8?

E147. Whom did FDR call "The Father of the United Nations?"

E148. What led to a very substantial increase in the population of western Canada in the 19th Century?

E149. What nation gained its independence from the USSR on September 23, 1991?

E150. The anniversary of whose death was officially named "Primrose Day" in his honor?

E151. Which explorer died of dysentery on board his ship the *Defiance* in 1596?

E152. Who led the second Francophone Rebellion of 1885?

E153. Which US inventor published the *Grand Trunk Herald*, the first newspaper ever printed on a train, at the age of 12?

E154. What scientist and pacifist wrote *Why War?*

E155. What statute created full self-government for Canada in 1931?

E156. Who was known as "L'ambassadeur electrique?"

E157. Who paid the Nazi government £20,000 to allow Sigmund Freud to come to England?

E158. What agreement, which failed to become law, promised Quebec freedom to remain a "distinct society" linguistically and culturally?

E159. What nation that once had two official languages now has eleven?

Did You Know?

- 182,000 of the 581,942 bridges in the United States are rated unsafe for traffic.

- A starfish can turn its stomach inside out.

- Nine million people were killed during World War I. The worldwide movement of troops to fight the war provided the distribution system for the influenza pandemic that followed the war. The pandemic killed 20 million.

- Edgar Allan Poe and LSD advocate Timothy Leary were both expelled from West Point.

- A snowflake contains about 100 crystals of ice.

- John Wilkes Booth shot Lincoln in a theater and was found in a warehouse. Lee Harvey Oswald shot Kennedy from a warehouse and was found in a theater.

- In 1998 the US Senate passed an amendment to the tobacco bill that would limit the amount lawyers can get for tobacco suit litigation to $4000.00 per hour. (That's four thousand dollars per hour, folks)

- T.H. Huxley coined the word "agnosticism."

- Recent studies have suggested that the Milky Way Galaxy is older than the universe itself.

- "Dixie," the Southern army's marching and camp song, was written by a Northerner.

- The word alcohol comes from the Arabic word, al-kuhl, meaning "a powder for painting the eyelids."

- Because people threw their garbage in the streets, the "Black Death" of the 14th Century killed nearly half of the population

- Before birth, infants experience sexual arousal.

- The smallest shark is six inches long.

- The only problem with death is its finality.

E160. What government department administered Yellowstone National Park from 1872 to 1916?

E161. What is the largest elected legislative body in the world?

E162. What was the first country to officially recognize the United States in 1776?

E163. Between AD 270-283, how many Roman emperors were chosen by the army?

E164. Pepin the Short was the first ruler of what dynasty?

E165. Which Norman English king ruled from 1135-1154?

E166. How many words were in Washington's second inaugural address?

E167. In what year were US patents first offered?

E168. What historic figure was sent about 1500 virgins from whom to choose a bride?

E169. What assassin yelled, "Sic semper tyrannis?"

E170. Who was "Bloody Mary?"

E171. What is this clue that helped detectives capture a suspect in a major crime: 4U13.41?

E172. Which English monarch had 17 children and yet left no heir to the throne?

E173. Name the governor who tried to save Richard Hauptmann's life?

E174. Which English monarch died without heirs, thus bringing forth the Stuarts?

E175. Who were "The Airman" and "The Carpenter?"

E176. In what years were no Nobel Prizes awarded?

E177. The IMF has classified how many nations as "advanced economies?"

E178. What country has the lowest Gross National Product (GNP)?

E179. What other name is Gaius Julius Caesar Germanicus known by?

E180. What US public official was born in Havana, Cuba, and founded Astro Dynamics in 1960?

E181. What was the former name of the Brooklyn Bridge?

E182. What was the former name of "Camp David," the retreat of US presidents?

E183. Since what year have all popes been cardinals?

E184. How many hours and minutes did Charles Lindbergh's flight across the Atlantic take?

E185. Fill in the blanks to find the name of a civilian WWII hero:

_ A _ U _   _ _ _ L E _ _ E _ _

PC60: Who is this writer?

PC61: Who is the subject
of this sculpture?

PC62: Name this pro baseball player.

PC63: What is the name
of this artist?

PC64: What type of bird is this?

PC65: Who is this musician?

PC66: Name this actor.

PC67: In what film does
this scene appear?

PC68: What are these medals?

PC69: This scene is from what film?

PC70: In what TV series
do you see this symbol?

PC71: What North American city is this?

PC72: From what year in the 1990s is this New York Mets yearbook?

PC73: Who is this Canadian personality?

PC74: Who is this man?

PC75: Who is this young man?

F: GEOGRAPHY

Did You Know?

- It is believed that Shakespeare was 46 years old around the time the King James version of the Bible was written. In Psalm 46, the 46th word is shake and the 46th word from the last word is spear.

- 6,000,000 middle and upper class families have moved out of America's urban centers since 1970.

- During World War II, 20 million backyard and city rooftop victory gardens produced 50% of America's vegetables.

- In a standard 52-card deck of cards, there are 2,598,960 possible hands of five cards.

- In their version of football, the Matami tribe of West Africa use a human skull as their ball.

- On June 25, 1630, the fork was introduced to the American dinner table.

F1. Where will you find Djakovica, Pristina, & Pec?

F2. Where will you find the Emmons and Ingraham Glaciers?

F3. In what US city are Forsyth Park and Colonial Park Cemetery?

F4. As of 1998 what is the only US state capital without a McDonald's?

F5. What is the southernmost tip of Africa?

F6. Routes 3, 7, 103, 107, and 118 lead to what North American city?

F7. If you are standing at the corner of Rr. Myslym Shyri and Bulevardi Deshmoret e Kombit, what city are you in?

F8. What 13 world capitals begin with the letter B?

F9. What is the deepest station in the London Underground System?

F10. In what US city will you find Windsor Beach, Crazy Horse Campground and Rotary Park Beach?

F11. What is the highest city in Africa?

F12. The coastline of which geographic location is 18,950 miles?

F13. In what city is Sangster International Airport?

F14. How many countries of the world have a population of over 100 million?

F15. What is the world's largest lake?

F16. What is the only African nation to rank in the top ten nations in population?

F17. What is "Communism Peak?"

F18. What else is *Godwin Austen* called?

F19. What is Asia's largest island?

F20. Other than the Mississippi-Missouri, what is the North American river to rank in the list of the world's 14 longest rivers?

F21. In terms of area, what are the two smallest continents in the world?

F22. What continent has no permanent population?

F23. How many nations are bisected by the equator?

F24. South Georgia Island is located in what body of water?

F25. What is the deepest part of the Indian Ocean called?

F26. What is Kalaallit Nunaat?

F27. To the North is Edmonton, to the East is Eirth, to the west is Isleworth, and to the south is Beckenham. What large city is in the middle?

F28. What nation covers more lines of latitude than any other?

F29. What is the "Firth of Forth?"

F30. 1:24,000 is an example of what type of cartographic scale?

F31. In the First Century AD, the Romans built the city of Turicum, which now is the site of what European city?

F32. Where is Finnmark?

F.33. What is the largest lake in Asia?

F34. What is the deepest sea in the world?

F35. What is Canada's largest lake?

F36. What is North America's largest reservoir?

F37. In terms of population, what is Europe's largest city?

F38. What non-African nation has the highest infant mortality rate?

F39. In population, what are Africa's two largest cities?

F40. How many cities in the USA have "Detroit" in their name?

F41. What country has a coastline of 151,492 miles?

F42. Fill in the blanks to discover the name of a city on the Sinai Peninsula that could also be called a talking waterway:

_ _ _ _   _ _ l _

F43. What is South America's highest mountain?

F44. By the year 2000, what urban area is expected to have a population of nearly 30 million?

F45. What's the largest mountain in Pakistan?

F46. What is Europe's largest waterfall?

F47. What nation has the following ethnic groups: Baoule (23%), Bete (18%), and Senoufou (15%)?

F48. Japan is bounded by which four bodies of water?

F49. The Gilbert Islands are part of what nation?

F50. What is Europe's largest island?

Did You Know?

- The character of the Mad Hatter in *Alice in Wonderland* is actually based upon the hat makers in towns of the 1880s. The large felt hats of the day had supports made from mercury, which created an organic form of psychosis, causing them to be declared crazy.

- Las Vegas has more unlisted telephone numbers than any other US city.

- In the USA there are 18 doctors named Dr Doctor and one named Dr Surgeon. There is a dermatologist named Dr Rash, a psychiatrist named Dr Couch, and an anesthesiologist named Dr Gass.

- It took 47 days before the Museum of Modern Art realized it had hung a Matisse painting upside down.

- Illinois is the US state with the most personalized license plates.

- The memory of a goldfish is 3 seconds.

F51. What is the lowest point in Africa?

F52. What is Australia's highest mountain?

F53. What South American country touches borders with more countries than any other on the continent?

F54. What nation has 1% arable land?

F55. As of 1997, the estimated population of which nation was 31,389?

F56. What nation comprises more than 1200 islands, of which about 220 are inhabited?

F57. What nation's ethnic groups are primarily Mestizo and Amerindian?

F58. The Arab-Berber ethnic group makes up 99% of which nation?

F59. What is the only official Hindu kingdom in the world?

F60. What is the northernmost nation to claim ownership of part of Antarctica?

F61. What is the only US state to border only one other state?

F62. What world capital is built on nine islands connected by bridges?

F63. What are parallels and meridians also called?

F64. When meridians become straight lines that intersect at the contact point and parallels are seen as concentric circles, what type of map projection are we looking at?

F65. What is the largest island in the Norwegian Sea?

F66. How many nations touch the Gulf of Bothnia?

F67. Each degree of latitude is equal to approximately how many miles?

F68. What is the only European nation to rank in the top ten nations in population?

F69. How many cities of any size in the world have "Philadelphia" in their name?

F70. What is the world's second largest desert?

F71. What is the largest lake in the United States?

F72. What is Canada's largest island?

F73. Fill in the blanks and give us the name of the country that is known as the:

     _ A _ E _ A _   _ O   _ _ U T _
                    _ _ E _ I _ _

F74. What country's name is derived from a Mayan word that means "muddy waters?"

F75. In area, what is the largest county in the United States?

F76. What islands were once called the "Fortunate Islands" or "Isles of the Blest?"

F77. What city lays at the head of the Pearl River?

F78. How many California cities have a population over 100,000?

F79. What present day city stands where the Berber village of Anfa stood in the 12th Century?

F80. What US city is in the heart of a fertile area called the Piedmont and is one of the nation's largest textile centers?

F81. Where are both "Cleopatra's Needles" now located?

F82. What is the world's lowest river?

F83. Fill in the blanks to find the name of 288 verdant acres in
London:

_ _ _   _ _ R _ _ _ S

F84. Which explorer gave California the names of San Diego,
Santa Barbara, Monterey, and Carmel, among others?

F85. What islands get their name from the Spanish word "cayo,"
meaning rock or islet?

F86. What city is capital of the Hyogo Prefecture?

F87. What island, which was severely damaged by an earthquake in
1964, is home to a US Coast Guard base?

F88. What world capital is highest in elevation?

F89. What US capital city was settled along the Grand River
in the 1830s?

F90. What is France's second largest port city?

F91. What county is located in the province of Munster and
comprises most of the Golden Vale?

F92. What city stands on seven hills and was discovered by ancient
explorers who sailed up the Tagus River?

F93. Fill in the blanks and give us the name of the city
whose nickname is:

_ H _   _ _ T _   _ F   S _ I _ S

Did You Know?

- February 1865 was the only month in recorded history with no full moon.
- About 10% of the population is left-handed.
- The first opera was *Dafne*.
- Theodor Herzl, the Zionist leader who was born on May 2, 1860, once had the astonishing idea of converting Jews to Christianity as a way of combating anti-Semitism.
- The relative average walking speed of pedestrians is affected by the size of the city. All over the world, the larger the city, the faster people walk.
- There are 206 bones in the adult human skeleton.
- The first airplane races were held in Reims, France, in 1909, and 28 of the 38 entrants crashed.
- About one-third of all deaths from cancer are attributed to smoking.

F94. In 1848, the population of San Francisco was 800. What was the population in 1850?

F95. In 1781, what was the Spanish name for what would become Los Angeles?

F96. What European city is located on the Maseta plateau?

F97. What city was founded in 1671 and given the name Nueva Zamora?

F98. Which republic comprises two parallel chains of coral atolls 800 miles long?

F99. What are the five parts or "seas" of the Mediterranean Sea?

F100. What major US city was a small village in 1896, consisting of a few dwellings situated around Fort Dallas?

F101. What is Italy's greatest railway city?

F102. What nation is known to Arabs as al-Maghreb al-Aqsa or "farthest west?"

F103. Before Moscow, what was Russia's capital city?

F104. The main tributaries of which river are the Darling and Murrumbidgee?

F105. The Netherlands has how many provinces?

F106. What European city is divided into 20 governmental units and further divided for a total of 80 quaters?

F107. What British institution is located on Victoria Street, with its main entrance at 10 Broadway?

F108. In area, what is Europe's largest country?

F109. Whose city motto is *contemnit procellas*?

F110. What capital city is named for a tribe of Athabascan Indians who used a certain color copper to make their tools?

F111. What city in the Russian language means "ruler of the east?"

PC76: What is this Western Hemisphere city?

PC77: Name the make, year and model of this car.

PC79: Name this actress.

PC78: Who is this criminal?

PC81: Who is this author?

PC80: Name this young actor.

PC82: Name this Pinter play.

PC83: Name this early Rock 'n' Roll star.

PC84: Name this R&B, country, folk and rock star.

PC85: What European city is this?

PC87: What armed forces unit
wears this patch?

PC86: Name this
pro baseball player.

PC88: Who is this composer?

PC89: Name this young actor.

PC90: What is this European city?

G: SPORTS, LEISURE & GAMES

G1. Who are the NHL rookies to have scored 50 or more goals?

G2. Of the NHL, NBA, MLB, and NFL, what teams have names that don't end in "s" ?

G3. Who is Terry Bollea otherwise known as?

G4. Who was the first non-rookie to score more than 50 goals in an NHL season?

G5. Who holds the world record for running 100 yards backward?

G6. Who shouted "Ma, he's killing me!" in the middle of a world title boxing fight?

G7. Where does the term "love" come from as used in tennis for zero?

G8. How many feet separate the head pin from the foul line in bowling?

G9. Who filed a lawsuit against Adidas, claiming he was forced to stitch together World Cup '98 soccer balls in a Chinese labor camp?

G10. How much money did Scottie Pippen earn from the Chicago Bulls during the 1997-98 season?

G11. What professional basketball team won 11 championships in 13 years?

G12. Who won a United States Open golf title and then the following year finished tied for 60th place in the same competition?

ENTRY DEADLINE: September 12, 2000

G13. Who receives the Conn Smythe Trophy?

G14. What was the actual site of the ancient Olympic games?

G15. Who holds the major league baseball record for most home runs hit in the month of June?

G16. How many stitches are there on a major league baseball?

G17. How many ties were there for the NCAA National Football Champions?

G18. What is the official name of the World Cup?

G19. Who holds the record for most goals scored in a World Cup tournament?

G20. What do these names represent: *Magic, Columbia, Sappho, Madeleine, Mischief, Resolute*?

G21. Name the two women who have won five US Figure Skating Championships.

G22. What are the two sites in the USA that have hosted the Winter Olympics?

G23. How long in miles is the Indianapolis Motor Speedway?

G24. How many shutouts have there been in the Rose Bowl games?

G25. What is located at Nall Avenue at 63rd Street in Mission, Kansas?

G26. What are the four major pro golf tournaments?

Did You Know?

- Lynyrd Skynyrd was the name of the gym teacher of the boys who went on to form that successful band. He once told them, "You boys ain't never gonna amount to nothin'."
- By the year 2020, the average age of people will be 42.
- The mosquito is responsible for more human deaths in the world than any other living thing.
- The earth weighs about 13 septillion, 176 sextillion pounds.
- A duck's quack does not echo.
- There are more living organisms on the skin of a single human being than there are human beings on the surface of the earth.

G27. Who is the leading PGA career money winner?

G28. Fill in the blanks to find a three-word formal thoroughbred:

     _ _ A C _   _ _ E   _ F _ A _ _

G29. What NFL team had the very first #1 draft pick?

G30. Which NFL kicker has nine touchdowns?

G31. What company was acquitted of attempting to defraud a Lloyd's of London insurance syndicate out of $350,000 for a cancelled 1991 boxing match?

G32. Where and when was the first professional basketball game played?

G33. What team scored the most points in the history of the Cotton Bowl?

G34. Who holds the record for most points in a career in NCAA Division I-A football?

G35. How many overtime games were played between the final two teams in the NCAA Division I basketball championship finals?

G36. What college has won the most NCAA fencing championships?

G37. As of 1998, what team does Tara VanderVeer coach?

G38. What is the name of the apprentices who help goad the bull into charging at the matador?

G39. How many yards are in a marathon race?

G40. How many female competitors were there in the first modern Summer Olympics?

G41. What Indy 500 winner had the slowest time?

G42. What horse holds the record for the fastest Kentucky Derby and what was the time?

G43. What sport did the South Philadelphia Hebrew Association play?

G44. What team scored the most points in which Super Bowl game?

G45. What four categories comprise the NFL quarterback rating system?

G46. Other than proper names or nicknames, what are baseball's two double Bs?

G47. Who was the first DH to come to bat in the Major Leagues?

G48. What are the only two days of the year when there are never any scheduled professional sporting events (MLB, NFL, NBA, and NHL)?

G49. What are the only two countries to have competed in every modern Olympics?

G50. What is the most popular sport at American nudist camps?

G51. What sport is derived from Ga-Lahs?

G52. Why was the Hula Hoop banned in Japan in the 1950s?

G53. What do you call the large disk used in tiddlywinks?

G54. In a deck of cards, what four historical kings do the kings in the deck represent?

G55. Who is Barbara Millicent Roberts?

G56. How many white dots does Pac-Man have to eat on each board of the original arcade game?

G57. What did the Frankford Yellowjackets accomplish?

G58. In what Super Bowl game did Max McGee catch seven passes for 138 yards?

G59. What is the longest play in Super Bowl history?

G60. What organization introduced the three-point play in basketball?

G61. How many times have NBA teams won the world championship by four games to none?

G62. Who are the four NBA players who tied for Rookie of the Year honors?

G63. Fill in the blanks to get a winning hand:

_ C _ _   _ _ L _

G64. What is the oldest trophy competed for by professional athletes in North America?

G65. An influenza epidemic stopped what two cities from completing the Stanley Cup playoff?

G66. Who is "Cool Papa?"

G67. Fill in the blanks to find out what you call a score of 26 in Darts:

_ _ D   _ _ D   _ _ E _ _ F _ _ T

G68. What former snooker champion had only one good eye?

G69. What is the highest number of moves ever recorded between any piece without being captured in a game of chess?

G70. How many dimples are on a regulation golf ball?

G71. What college has won the most consecutive NCAA gymnastics titles?

Did You Know?

- Whales increase in weight 30,000,000,000 times in their first two years.

- The female orgasm is a powerful painkiller because it is concomitant with the release of endorphins

- The Space Shuttle's main engine weighs $1/7^{th}$ as much as a train engine, but delivers as much horsepower as 39 train engines.

- Koalas never drink water. They get fluids from the eucalyptus leaves they eat.

- The potato is the most widely grown vegetable in the world. About 1.4 million acres of land in the US are used to produce potatoes each year. About 70% of these potatoes are produced in the northern regions of the country, namely Idaho, North Dakota, Minnesota, Maine and Washington state. The annual value of the US crop is estimated to be nearly $3 billion.

G72. What was the last Ivy League college to win the NCAA ice hockey championship?

G73. What college has won more NCAA wrestling titles than any other?

G74. In one year, who earned the most money in the PBA?

G75. What is the minimum age to enter the Senior PGA Tour?

G76. What is the complete, official name of the Wimbledon Grand Slam event?

G77. What have Bernard Hinault and Miguel Indurain accomplished that no one else has?

G78. Fill in the blanks to discover a person very familiar with queens and kings:

_ N _ T O _ _   _ A _ _ _ V

G79. What did Molla Bjurstedt accomplish?

G80. What horse won the Eclipse Award five years in a row?

G81. Who is the only Penn State University football player to be a number one pick in the NFL draft?

G82. Who holds the NFL record for the highest career rushing average?

G83. In Super Bowl history, which kicker missed what would have been the winning field goal with eight seconds remaining in the game?

G84. Who has played in more NBA games than anyone else?

G85. Which two players have scored the most points in NBA history?

G86. How many franchises did the NHL start with?

G87. Who donated the Stanley Cup?

G88. Who has played more major league baseball games than any other player?

G89. Who was the last Triple Crown winner in major league baseball?

G90. How much money do you receive if you win the Hart Trophy?

G91. Who selects MLB's MVP?

Did You Know?

- According to Information Week, the annual productivity loss by US business due to employees playing computer games is an estimated $100 billion – which works out to 2% of the Gross Domestic Product.

- Architects receive the Pritzker Prize.

- A woman proudly wearing a valuable pearl necklace is actually displaying an entombed parasitic worm, not a coated grain of sand. The free, spherical pearl is produced when the larvae from a parasitic flatworm, which comes from seabirds, burrows inside the oyster to begin the process.

- By the year 2025, there will be eight billion people living on the planet.

G92. Who won the first Cy Young award?

G93. What two men cancelled the World Series because they refused to have their team play a team from an "inferior league?"

G94. Fill in the blanks to find out which MLB manager has the highest career winning percentage:

_ O _   _ _ C _ _ T _ Y

G95. Who drove in the most runs in a World Series?

G96. Who is the only real person to be ever featured as a Pez dispenser?

G97. Who invented Lincoln Logs?

G98. Why is it illegal to sell an *E.T.* doll in France?

G99. Who hit a home run at his first at-bat in college, the Olympics, and in the major leagues?

G100. What is the only USA city where all of the professional teams have the same colors on their uniforms?

G101. Who is the only player to have died as a result of an injury received in a major league baseball game?

G102. What is the most expensive property in a British Monopoly set?

G103. What was the first US pro football team to have emblems on its helmets?

G104. What is the oldest continually held sports event in the USA?

G105. What is the sport with the highest ratio of officials to participants?

G106. Who was the first PGA pro player to win a tournament using a colored ball?

G107. Who is major league baseball's all time leader with a career batting average of .367?

G108. Whose all time career earned run average is 1.82?

G109. What city holds the "Oldsmobile Classic?"

G110. What is the "Miracle of Coogan's Bluff?"

G111. What is the record for fewest points scored in an NBA game with a shot clock?

G112. Which NCAA Division I-A running back has more career carries than any other?

G113. Which NCAA Division I-A quarterback has the highest career passing percentage?

G114. What NCAA Division I basketball championship team scored the highest number of points in a game and what was that figure?

G115. What college has won more NCAA water polo titles than any other?

G116. Who convened the series of meetings that led to the formation of the NCAA?

G117. What college won the first NCAA Division I basketball championship?

G118. How many male competitors were there in the first modern Summer Olympics?

G119. How many horses have won the Triple Crown?

G120. In the year Bjorn Borg won the French Open, which player won all the other Grand Slam events?

G121. Fill in the blanks to discover a "strong" part of any baseball stadium:

_ O _ _ R   _ _ L E _

G122. What West Coast US college sports teams are nicknamed the "Matadors?"

G123. Fill in the blanks to find a "nice smelling" race:

_ U _   _ O _   T _ _   _ O _ E _

G124. Who is Chamique Holdsclaw?

G125. What college team has won more NCAA indoor track championships than any other?

G126. What two cities gain NHL franchises in the year 2000 and how much money will each have to pay to enter?

G127. What major league baseball team has had more Rookies of the Year than any other?

G128. In what years were two All Star baseball games played?

G129. Every major league baseball player eligible for the Hall of Fame with 3,000 hits or more is in the Hall of Fame except for what player?

G130. What sport was invented by the physical director of the YMCA in Holyoke, Massachusetts?

G131. What Philadelphia-born baseball player wrote the autobiography, *It's Good to Be Alive?"*

G132. In Europe, what activity are your undertaking if you belong to the FICC?

G133. Who was known as the father of modern camping and created the Association of Cycle Campers in Berkshire, England?

Did You Know?

- The earth's magnetic field completely reverses itself every few hundred million years and no one knows why.

- Hitler was a hypochondriac, taking as many as 28 types of medication, including injections from bulls' testicles.

- The penis contains no fat.

- According to the D & B report, the US loses an estimated 6 million jobs per year due to information stolen through industrial espionage. The annual US revenue loss due to information stolen through industrial espionage is estimated at $200 billion.

- Contrary to popular belief, Galileo did not invent the telescope. It was invented by Hans Lippershey in 1608, but Galileo did make significant improvements on it.

- More than 300,000,000 sperm cells are ejaculated during an orgasm.

- TV broadcasts actually got their start in Britain in 1937 when the BBC transmitted the coronation of King George VI. The first US broadcast was at the 1939 World's Fair.

- James Whistler, the US painter, told everyone he spoke French fluently, but at a restaurant he asked his friend to order for him after he ordered a "flight of stairs."

- John Adams estimated that at the time of the American Revolution only a third of the population supported the revolution while an equal third continued to support the British Crown. The remaining third didn't much care either way. Almost as many colonists fought on the side of the British as against them.

G134. Which US tennis player's parents fled Communist China?

G135. What board game was called Tric-Trac by the French and Germans in the 17th Century?

G136. How many squares are there on a Scrabble® board?

G137. Who wrote the first manual of chess instruction in 1561?

G138. What board game was invented by a Germantown, Pennsylvania, man based upon his family's favorite resort spot?

G139. What pastime uses objects such as the Malay, three-sticker, and the box?

G140. What football position did Vince Lombardi play in college?

G141. What game has the following terms: Shooters, Cloudies, and Cat's Eyes?

G142. What form of physical combat literally means "the art of empty hands?"

G143. In model railroads, what is the smallest scale (smallest size)?

G144. The National Rife Association was formed in Britain in what year?

G145. What game has a court size of six feet wide and 52 feet long, with an actual playing surface of 39 feet long?

G146. What race is 1,137 miles long?

G147. What sport has a goalkeeper, three forwards, and three backs?

G148. In what sport are these following numbers relevant: 118, 126, 134, 142, 150, 158, 167, 177, and 190?

G149. What move do you make in chess under the following notation: P—KN4?

PC91: Who is this author?

PC92: In what film will you see this shot?

PC93: Who is this young man who later created sci-fi epics?

PC94: Who is this actress?

PC95: Who is this early TV comic?

PC96: What company has this logo?

PC97: Who is this
pro baseball player?

PC98: Name these characters.

PC99: In what film will you
find this shot?

PC100: Name this physicist.

PC101: Name this
pro baseball player.

PC102: In what film
does this scene appear?

PC103: Who was born here?

PC105: Name this 1950s
and 1960s pop music group.

PC104: Who is this
pro baseball pitcher?

PC106: Name this film
and the character.

H: MISCELLANEOUS

Did You Know?

- The human being has about 2,500,000 sweat glands.
- Fear of the number 13 has its roots in the Last Supper of Jesus, where there were 13 persons, one of whom a traitor.
- Tattoos date back to 2000 BC, where they have been found on mummies. They have been used throughout history to ward off evil or to denote high rank.
- People cry when they laugh very hard as they are putting pressure on the muscles of the eyes that squeeze the lachrymal glands, which produce tears.
- During the Vietnam War, the US employed this euphemism for its bombing raids — "protective reaction strikes."
- Metonymy is the use of one word for another similar word or phrase, such as, "A spokesman for the Pentagon said today ..." Pentagon is used rather than Department of Defense.
- The average life of a wart is three to four months, but some can persist for years while spawning satellite warts in other parts of the body.

H1. What is tmesis?

H2. What was the distress call used from 1904 to 1906, which preceded "S.O.S?"

H3. What is the highest scoring word in the English language that one can use in a Scrabble® game?

H4. What is a parthenophobic?

H5. How many letters are there between A and Z in the English alphabet?

H6. What is the longest single-word palindrome in the English language?

H7. What is a bruxomaniac?

H8. What is a "gandy dancer?"

H9. What word in the English language has the most definitions?

H10. As of May 1998, what is the only international airline never to have crashed?

H11. Who invented the lava lamp?

H12. What city and state is the location of the office of Christian conservative Ralph Reed?

H13. What newspaper chain owns the *Miami Herald, Detroit Free Press, San Jose Mercury News, Philadelphia Inquirer*, etc?

H14. Whose AOL username was "Boysrch?"

H15. Infiniti is a division of what corporation?

H16. In what city will you find the newspaper *Kompas*?

H17. What do Gilbert K. Davis and Joseph Cammarata have in common?

H18. What is known as the *Deux Chevaux*?

H19. Taken as a whole, what do the following refer to:
MS-70, MS-60, AU-50, VF-30?

H20. What is "RE-FI?"

H21. Who first publicly coined the word: "agnosticism?"

H22. What's the name of the 110 square mile lake in California that is the worst source of pollution in the United States?

H23. What is the name of the exorcist of the Notre Dame cathedral in Paris?

H24. In what US city will you find the UAW and Chevrolet highways?

H25. What is the brand name of the fat-free cooking oil olestra?

H26. What is located at 7701 Legacy Drive, Plano, TX 75024?

H27. What US state's citizens experience the highest busy rate when trying to call the National Cancer Institute?

H28. What company slogan is "Work Hard. Fly Right?"

H29. Fill in the blanks to find out what nation receives about 37% of Washington state's wheat exports:

_ _ _ I S _ _ N

H30. What is the name of the first brokerage firm with a seat on the New York Stock Exchange to issue shares to the public?

H31. An extension of the Morris K. Udall Foundation, what is the name of the US institute to mediate environmental disputes?

H32. What company produces the *Smart Suite—Millennium Edition*?

H33. What is the *Beige Book*?

H34. Fill in the blanks to find the name of the managing editor of one of America's prestigious newspapers who has written books about the SEC, India, and Getty Oil:

_ _ _ _ E   _ _ L _

H35. Who started Gateway 2000?

H36. What is the "Unifying Voice for Advertising?"

H37. What goes on in the mind of Slobodan Milosevic? (Any answer will do — literally.)

H38. What happened to CEO Al Dunlap in 1998?

H39. Fill in the blanks to find out who are the 15,000 people that manage about 200,000 events each day which help you get where you are going:

_ _ _   _ R _ _ _ _ C   _ O _ T _ _ _ L _ R _

H40. What is Oswiecim?

H41. What is California's state medical program called?

H42. What is the meaning of the word *karojisatsu*?

H43. What is IOLTA?

H44. On what date did the Dow fall 207.01 points to 8,627.93?

H45. What is the name of the Bishop of Chiapas?

H46. Road Runner is a joint venture of which two companies?

H47. What company owns Toys'R'Us?

H48. What does the EOE Index measure?

H49. John H. Johnson heads what major magazine?

H50. What is physcrophilia?

H51. What is the word for the ball of food your tongue creates while chewing?

H52. What is the word for a solid object with nine sides?

H53. What word means the art of collecting ties?

H54. What are the three newest letters in the English language?

H55. What South America connection is shared by G. Richard Wagoner Jr and Mark T. Hogan?

H56. Fill in the blanks to find the name of a newsworthy visitor from Britain to the USA:

_ _   P _ _ R   _ O U _ _ E   _ O O _ _ A R _

H57. Who is the founder of Hyundai?

H58. The Inter-American Commission on Human Rights is part of what organization?

H59. Fill in the blanks to find a person with a few dollars to spare:

_ I _ _   _ _ T _ S

H60. In advertising, what is the "up-front market?"

H61. Who is head of Virgin Group?

H62. What and where is the *Criterion Brasserie*?

H63. What is the Drozdy Complex?

H64. What is the "Sacred Grove of Zeus?"

H65. A lens is so named because it resembles what?

H66. What is a "Gift Economy?"

H67. What are Switzerland's three largest banks?

H68. What did workers of Ravenswood Hospital Medical Center refuse to do in May 1988?

H69. How many members are there in the Czech Republic's parliament?

H70. What US airport can you approach by using Interstates 94, 55, and 294?

H71. Among these listed what is the least busy airport: Dallas/Ft Worth, Detroit Metro Wayne, Minneapolis-St Paul, Orlando International, or Philadelphia International?

H72. According to the *Koran*, how many times a day should one pray?

H73. Fill in the blanks to find a thing that provides higher support:

   _ C _ _ _ O L _ _ N G

Did You Know?

- The aardvark (the Dutch word for "earth pig") has claws so strong and sharp that it can open termite mounds that humans can only break into with a pickax.
- Puberty begins from 11-14 years of age and lasts up to the age of 24 in some cases.
- The first money coins were developed in 7Th Century BC by the city-state of Lydia in Asia Minor. They were made of gold and silver.
- The first painting to show eyeglasses was in 1352 by Tommaso de Modena.
- McDonald's and Kentucky Fried Chicken were both founded in 1955.
- Legal holidays in Canada are called "Statutory Days."

H74. What is Europe's tallest building?

H75. What is the telephone country code for Azerbaijan?

H76. Collectively, what do these letters represent: Csb, Aw, Dfb, BWh?

H77. Within five, how many nations report Jewish people as part of their population?

H78. What city is headquarters for the World Council of Churches?

H79. Where will you find "brickfielder winds?"

H80. What is this book's ISBN?

H81. What was Houdini's real name?

H82. Fill in the blanks to find a five-word phrase that everyone ought to have:

A   _ _ O _   _ E _ S _   O _   _ _ M O R

H83. What nation's telephone country code is 4175?

H84. What was the costliest hurricane in US history in terms of lives lost?

H85. As of 1996, what did this number represent: 5,772,351,000?

H86. Pascal and blanched are what types of vegetable?

H87. What two US states have the most hazardous waste sites?

H88. In the 1980s, which newspaper received the most Pulitzer Prizes for national reporting?

H89. Where will you find "mistral winds?"

H90. What is an octothorpe?

H91. How long is a jiffy?

H92. How many letters are there in the Hawaiian alphabet?

H93. What two words in the English language have all the vowels in order?

H94. Fill in the blanks to discover the phobia you have from fear of getting peanut butter stuck to the roof of your mouth:

_ R _ C _ I _ U T _ _ _ P H O B I A

H95. Where are the "williwaw winds" found?

H96. What newspaper received the first Pulitzer Prize for editorial writing?

H97. Who married his cousin Emma Wedgwood in 1839?

H98. Whose earlier jobs were with the James Flower & Brothers Machine Shop and the Detroit Dry Dock Company?

H99. Who was not the founder of the *Saturday Evening Post*, even though the magazine's masthead claims so?

H100. Whose sisters, Roisa, Mitzi, and Paula were gassed at Auschwitz?

H101. What Soviet leader owned nine Rolls-Royces?

H102. What US president owned a cat named Tabby and a dog named Fido?

H103. Who was buried in an unmarked pauper's communal grave in St Mark's Church, Vienna, in 1791?

H104. What word in the English language has all the vowels in reverse order?

H105. What is Yoshida Kogyo Kabushibibaisha?

H106. What was the original color of the White House in Washington DC?

H107. What US manufacturer said: "Exercise is bunk. If you are healthy, you don't need it; if you are sick, you shouldn't take it?"

H108. How many steps lead to the top of the Leaning Tower of Pisa?

H109. Fill in the blanks to discover the chief export of Nauru:
_ I R _   _ R O _ _ I N _ S

H110. Who said: "Sometimes a cigar is just a cigar?"

H111. What two organizations own the most land in New York City?

H112. Who is patron saint of bricklayers?

H113. Who was the first Ronald McDonald?

H114. What plant did Sigmund Freud fear?

H115. What did Karen Creamo invent?

H116. Fill in the blanks to find the name of the candy bar named after a president's daughter:
_ _ _ Y   R _ _ _

H117. Who were blueberry Jelly Bellies created for?

H118. What is an alligator pear?

H119. In a recipe, how many drops are in a dash?

H120. Who smoked about 20 cigars a day and later in life had 33 operations for cancer?

H121. What is 2:10 pm to 3:35 pm?

H122. How much fluid can a ten gallon hat hold?

H123. Whose motto is: *Das beste oder nichts*?

H124. How many holes did William Hall drill into his own head in 1982 to kill himself successfully?

H125. What is the state gem of Alaska?

H126. What was originally defined as 1/ 10,000,000th of the distance from the equator to the poles?

H127. What company was first known as the Computing-Tabulating-Recording Corporation?

H128. What is the only non-human animal whose evidence is admissible in a US court?

H129. What US state has a Paradise and a Hell?

H130. What is the only example of a US state and its capital that do not share any letters?

H131. What is the equivalent Spanish acronym for UFO?

H132. Where is America's largest rosary?

H133. What was the brand name of the first product to have a UPC bar code on its packaging?

H134. Where would you find an ideo-locator?

H135. What is the only train in the New York subway system that does not travel to Manhattan Island?

H136. What are the only six entities to have appeared on the covers of *Time*, *Newsweek*, and *Sports Illustrated*?

H137. Where is the world's largest double-decker tram fleet?

H138. What has the distinct zip code: 12345?

H139. What are the only US radio call letters to spell out the name of its city or town?

H140. Fill in the blanks to discover this word, which would be forgotten if you had it:

_ E _ H _ L O _ I _ A

H141. What six nations have birds on their flag?

H142. Who was the only person to letter in four sports at UCLA?

H143. What astronaut's mother's maiden name was Moon?

H144. Fill in the blanks to find out what Alfred E. Neuman and David Letterman have in common:

_ _ A S _ _ M _

H145. What is the Egyptian hieroglyph for the number 100,000?

H146. Who was Ralph Lifshitz?

H147. What fabric literally means "cloth of the king?"

H148. Who invented the Egg McMuffin?

H149. What company manufactures Cosopt?

H150. Fill in the blanks to find something shallow:

_ A _ _ O _

H151. Who met a dentist on AOL and then when the dentist was murdered became the beneficiary of a million dollar insurance policy?

H152. What does FASB stand for?

H153. What is the FTSE 100?

H154. What company is the world's largest steelmaker?

H155. What are astragalus roots, lablab beans, and cordyceps used for?

H156. Going "From Worst to First," which CEO turned a major airline around?

H157. What company owns BainBridgeBooks?

H158. In what city is the home office of Seagram Company?

H159. What is the name of Germany's largest bank?

H160. Within one percent, what is the average consumer credit card delinquency rate in the USA (which is defined as 30 days overdue for payments based upon 1997-98 statistics)?

H161. What does the Hang Seng Index measure?

H162. Fill in the blanks to find the name of a world political figure:

_ I _   _ _ E   _ U _ G

H163. Who was Matthew Eappen?

H164. What is the name of South Korea's news agency?

H165. Who was convicted of killing Bill Cosby's son, Ennis?

H166. What is USCEF?

H167. In what city is the headquarters for Poco Petroleum?

H168. On what exchange are cheddar cheese options traded?

H169. Which Northern Ireland group holds its annual parade on Garvaghy Road?

H170. What weighs 8.1 grams and is composed of outer layers of copper-nickel bonded to an inner core of pure copper, and has a diameter of 26.5 mm with a reeded edge?

H171. What Egyptian standard of linear measurement was used beginning in about 3000 BC?

H172. What country originated rye and bourbon whiskeys?

H173. What US college houses the Howard Hughes Medical Institute?

H174. What company owns Godiva Chocolatier?

H175. How many feet were in a Roman "pace?"

H176. What do these words describe: New York, Imperial, Great Lakes, Butterheads, and Paris White?

H177. What are 537.605 cubic inches called?

H178. Which university was chartered by Henry III in 1231?

H179. Who composed the music for the national anthem of Lesotho?

H180. What consists of a head, a tinder substance, and a handle?

H181. Fill in the blanks to find these "holy things" that have taken the country by storm:

_ A _ E _ S

H182. Fill in the blanks to find a five word expression that could be stated as "double fabricator hot dog burning:"

_ _ _ R   _ _ A _
_ A _ _ S   O _   _ I _ E

H183. Fill in the blanks to discover what you're probably doing right now:

S _ _ A _ C H _ _ G   Y _ _ R   _ _ A D

PC107: This scene is from what film?

PC108: What company placed
this early advertisement?

PC109: This symbol represents what
European transporation company?

PC110: Name this aircraft.

PC111: Who is this actress?

PC112: Name these two
20th Century people.

SUGGESTIONS & HINTS

The best advice we can offer is to take your time and do your research, and if you do that, you'll easily pass the Challenge. Forming a group with people knowledgeable about different subject categories is certainly a wise approach. There are some hints and actual answers to some questions scattered throughout this book, and we will offer a few hints on the website during the entire time frame of the Challenge. Visit www.transatlanticpub.com about once a month for news about the contest.

The following hints are either straight-forward, require a little thinking on your part, or are downright convoluted.

A2. O.V.E.D. A8. Temporary erection (i.e., at a fair or polling station). A33. The least obvious. A46. Copland. A110. You better put on deodorant. A154. Avian prisoner. A199. Liquid apprehension. A225. Tim Allen? No, not quite. A254. Partially Diana's last name. A311. It's something. B7. Three words. B38. A new kid on the block? B43. Al. B70. I'm trying to remember what happened. B116. Okay, a Jewish composer. B141.Less than 715. B159. A recent film. B191. Well, it's not the butler. B207. Nature's pretty things can't be all that bad. C3. Meet me there. C10. The firmament. C28. You don't have to be a monarch or a president to figure this one out. C38. It's free. C39. Think Europe. C72. Duh! C75. No more tube baby. D5.Viridisville. D32. That's some descent. D51. Tennessee Williams play. D105. Museum. D142. They like seeds. D177. Don't be too curious. E6. Very large and very quickly. E10. A mathematician. E21. It's not used cars, but it is used. E31. Think of the motherland. E50. Read the content.E79. It lasted 38 minutes. E104. He was armed to the teeth with evidence. E116. GST E169. "So Die All Tyrants!". F4. The state was once an independent country! F7. It's a capital. F23. Bisected: cutting through. F29. It's a cool name. No pun intended. F64. See a map teacher. G5. July 1983. G25. Rulemakers. G66. H-of-F-er. G96. Flag waver. G110. Check with some friends on the East Coast. G129. Wanna Bet? H4. "White" islands. H6. Some intrepid people own one. H26. Snacks. H42. Make absolutely certain you leave work on time. H50. Brrrr, yes! H53. It's up for... H66. Jim Mann. H97. What a species she was! H109. That's gross. H121. Sorry. H133. Chew on it for a while. H162. South... PC12. Afraid to fly. PC38. Detergent. PC43. Neighbors to the North. PC52. Disastrous fate for twenty years. PC56. Language is the key. PC60. Mr Knott. PC81. Little ones. PC84. Obscure liquid. PC96. On vacation.

More hints on the website, www.transatlanticpub.com, beginning about October 1, 1998 through July 2000.

About The Authors

Ronald P. Smolin has worked in public information capacities for the Prudential Insurance Company, City of Newark War on Poverty Program, and the New York City Human Resources Administration; and founded and is president of Trans-Atlantic Publications Inc. and Coronet Books Inc. He is a graduate of the Pennsylvania State University.

Anthony T. Notaro is a graduate of the University of Pennsylvania, with a double major in philosophy and intellectual history. He wishes to remain "as enigmatic as the questions in this book."

OFFICIAL ENTRY FORM   THE $25,000.00 CHALLENGE

ENTRY DEADLINE: SEPTEMBER 12, 2000

DATE: _____

YOUR NAME (Type or Print Clearly):_____

ORGANIZATION (IF ANY) _____

DATE OF BIRTH: _____   TYPE OF OCCUPATION: _____

ADDRESS: _____

CITY, STATE, ZIP or COUNTRY_____

(OPTIONAL) : E-mail or telephone number: _____

WE WILL NEVER DIVULGE YOUR PERSONAL INFORMATION TO ANY MARKETING OR MAIL ORDER FIRM

(OPTIONAL) If you are a student or someone who anticipates a possible move by the turn of the century, we advise providing us with a permanent address or telephone where you can be reached in case the address you provided is no longer valid. Enter that information here:

ENTERING THE CHALLENGE AS AN: _____ Individual   _____ Group

PLAYING WHICH CATEGORIES?   ALL_____   SOME_____(List letter(s) of categories)

(OPTIONAL) FICTITIOUS OR ACTUAL NAME: _____

(Note: You can call yourself or your group any name you wish, but please refrain from any profane name as it will be listed on our website.)

IF PART OF A GROUP, EACH MEMBER MUST SUBMIT AN OFFICIAL ENTRY FORM. THE GROUP LEADER IS THE ONE WE WILL CONTACT, SO PLACE THAT PERSON'S ENTRY FORM ON TOP AND MARK: "GROUP LEADER." Staple or band together the entry forms of all members of the group.

(OPTIONAL) CHARITY ALLOCATION

I OR WE ARE ASSIGNING _____% OF OUR WINNINGS TO THE FOLLOWING CHARITY, EDUCATIONAL INSTITUTION, OR OTHER NONPROFIT ORGANIZATION. Only one organization is permitted._____

(OPTIONAL) I or we are enclosing $2.00 US to cover the costs of receiving a complete listing of the answers to the Challenge approximately fourteen (14) days after the entry deadline of September 12, 2000.

_____ (Check if you have enclosed the $2.00) Group entries need only one $2.00 fee. The answers will be sent to the Group Leader's address. If members of the group want their own copies of the answers, check the line on your entry form and enclose $2.00.

READ THE FOLLOWING CONTEST RULES CAREFULLY:

1. Your answers to the questions must be typed or computer-generated. No handwritten responses will be accepted, and anyone submitting a handwritten entry will be disqualified. You MUST send your answers and entry forms by certified, return receipt mail no later than September 12, 2000, to qualify for the prize money. See address below.

2. Place the letter & question number before your response. Answer the questions to the Photo Challenge last, and place the letters "PC" before the number of your response. If you are entering in any particular category, make certain the letter of that category precedes your answers.

3. There are no fees to enter this contest.

4. Anyone from anywhere in the world is invited to try the Challenge, but in some rare cases, local or state laws may prohibit you from entering. Check your local laws, as the Publisher will not be responsible nor able to award prizes to those whose local or state laws prohibit entering a contest like this.

5. Any and all owners or employees (past, present, and future) of BainBridgeBooks, Trans-Atlantic Publications Inc., Coronet Books Inc. or subcontractors are prohibited from entering this contest, as well as their family, friends, and associates.

6. You must fill out the official entry form only found in this book, "The $25,000.00 Challenge." This cannot be photocopied.

7. For any group entering the contest, each member of that group must complete an official entry form and enclose it with the answers. The group leader's entry form should be on top and clearly marked: GROUP LEADER. (If you are entering on behalf of any organization, all members who are taking part in the Challenge must submit an official entry form. This is required to prevent any legal problems arising from prize money allocations.)

8. When answering questions, it is advisable to use the full name of a person or place to avoid any confusion, unless the last name is unique and singularly recognizable. Answers should be spelled correctly, however an occasional typo will not be penalized.

9. When you receive the answers to the Challenge and believe you have a more up-to-date response or a response you believe is the correct one, you can challenge the Publisher by sending a registered letter along with your documentation. If your challenge does not in any way affect the winners of the contest, then the Publisher will allocate the prize money accordingly, but recognize your challenge (if correct) on the website.

10. You may allocate any or all of your winnings to an educational, charitable or other nonprofit organization. These funds will be donated in your name(s), whether as an individual or as a group.

11. PRIZE TIERS: Whoever answers all questions correctly in all categories will receive the grand prize of $25,000.00 paid over a five-year period of $5,000.00 each year. If more than one person or group answers all the questions correctly, they will share the prize money equally for the five-year period. Payments will be made each January, beginning in 2001.

12. If no one answers all questions correctly, the next PRIZE TIER provides a $10,000.00 prize to the individual or group that has the most correct answers, providing they have answered sixty percent (60%) of all the questions correctly. This prize will be paid in two yearly amounts of $5,000.00. If more than one person or group answers the same amount of questions correctly, they will share the prize money equally for the two-year period.

13. Assuming no one has answered 100% of the questions correctly, the Publisher will award cash prizes of $1,000.00 to the five runners-up, i.e., to those coming in 2nd, 3rd, 4th, 5th, and 6th places after the winner of the $10,000.00 for most correct answers. (Remember, to qualify for any cash prize, you must answer at least 60% of the questions correctly.)

14. All entrants who answer correctly 60% of all the questions will receive a Trivia Challenge Certificate of Excellence suitable for framing. A Certificate will also be given to those who score the most points in any particular category.

15. The results of the contest will be posted on the Publisher's website on or about November 12, 2000. This listing will include the individual's or group's assigned Challenge Number, along with their fictitious or actual name if any. The complete set of answers to the Challenge will be posted on the website on or about December 1, 2000. Should there be no challenges nor unsettled disputes, awards will be allocated in January 2001.

16. Those entering this Challenge hold the Publisher harmless from unintentional mistakes or typographical errors and will not engage in litigation of any form unless there is substantial evidence of illegal activity by the Publisher.

17. All entries and/or correspondence must be sent by CERTIFIED, RETURN RECEIPT MAIL TO:

Trivia Challenge, BainBridgeBooks, 311 Bainbridge Street, Philadelphia PA USA 19147-1543

We cannot be held responsible if your entry does not reach us on time. It is advisable to submit the answers earlier as we will send acknowledgement.

18. Entrants should check the publisher's website at least once a month for news about possible clarifications of questions, hints to some questions, and other news about the challenge. If you do not have access to the Internet, please write the Publisher.

Website address: www.transatlanticpub.com (When the home page comes up, click on the Trivia Challenge book cover. You will be linked to an information site about the book. Click on the link to Trivia Challenge News.)

Notice: The book is protected under US and International copyright. Copying the material in this book is illegal and will result in the disqualification of the entrant.

ENTRANT: I have read and understood the rules of the $25,000.00 Challenge.

SIGNATURE: _____

CATEGORY SUMMARIES

Popular Entertainment
A = 319 questions

Arts & Humanities
B = 209 questions

Technology
C = 121 questions

The Sciences
D = 177 questions

History & Politics
E = 185 questions

Geography
F = 111

Sports & Leisure
G = 149

Miscellaneous
H = 183 questions

Photo Challenge
PC = 122 identifications

TOTAL QUESTIONS IN THE CHALLENGE: 1,566

PASSING GRADE: 940 or more answered correctly

(Certificates also given for most correct in any category)